QUICK and EASY NEWSLETTERS

How to spread the word about

your business, service, store,

association, non-profit, school,

library, sales network, club or family!

by **Elaine Floyd**

Dedicated to:

Alexandre B.,
Alexandre A.,
and
Alexandre M. Todorov

Also by Elaine Floyd:

Marketing With Newsletters
(EFG)

The Newsletter Editor's Handbook
(EFG, co-authored with Marvin Arth and Helen Ashmore)

Making Money Writing Newsletters
(EFG)

Creating Family Newsletters
(EFG)

Quick & Easy Newsletters: How to spread the word about your business, service, store, association, non-profit, school, library, sales network, club or family!

Acknowledgements: Lyn Dahl, newsletter seminar leader and world traveler, planted the idea for this project during a visit to the bayous of Louisiana. The book has been kept vibrant through the support and vision of great resellers like PaperDirect, Writer's Digest Books and referrals from readers like you. Thank you all.

Experience Required. This book assumes that you understand the basic operation of your Windows system and word processor—that you can locate files on a diskette, open them from within MS-Works, MS-Word, WordPerfect or MS-Publisher and save them on your computer and print them. It also assumes that you have your mailing list set up and can produce labels.

ISBN: 0-9630222-3-7

First Edition Update. First printing. Printed and bound in the USA.

Production Team:
MS-Word templates: Tim Celeski
Cartoons: Bradford Veley *(see page 143)*
Cover typography: Jim Weems, Ad Graphics
Cover photography & design: VIP Graphics

Published and distributed to the trade by:

quicknews@aol.com
www.newsletterinfo.com

LOOK INSIDE

Contents

While You're Turning the Page...

This is an example of the type of newsletter you'll be creating and the name used to describe each part. Ignore the words in parentheses for now.

Newsletter name
(News Name)

Tagline
(News Tagline)

Dateline
(News Tagline)

Nameplate

Section head
(News Section)

Headline
(News Headline)

News copy
(News Text)

Action line
(News Action)

Quotation
(News Quote)

Sidebar / Calendar
(News SB Text)

Attribution
(News Speaker)

Tips, Trends & Topics for Members of the Springfield Business Association   Summer 2003

BusinessBuzz

In Any Event

SMTWTFS

Annual Elections
7:00, August 30
Springfield Library Auditorium
Nominations are being taken for
open offices. (See related article)

Quarterly Meeting
Noon, July 1
Homestyle Banquet Center
Speaker: Mark Adams will discuss
how the Internet can help your
business.

Financing Seminar
7:00 - 10:00, July 14
YMCA Meeting Room #2
David Alexander, loan officer from
Springfield Savings Bank, discusses
financing options for small business
owners.

Electronics Expo
8:00 AM - 6:00 PM, July 14-18
Springfield Convention Center
Come and see the newest
developments in high-tech office
equipment.

Springfield Horse Show
5:00 PM - midnight, August 1-5
Springfield Fair Grounds
The business Association will have
a food booth at this annual event.
We're looking for people to work
the booth -- you'll probably get a
call from Tom Craddock.

Answer: Bowling

Hot Off the Presses

Mayor announces new civic center

Springfield will be getting a new multi-purpose civic center late next fall. The center will include a recreation center, a banquet facility, a conference center, and a library. Mayor Logan announced the project, which has been met with great enthusiasm by the Springfield community.

Use of the center's facility will be free for all Springfield residents. The recreation center will have a swimming pool, jogging track, gymnasium and fitness equipment. The banquet facility and conference center will be convenient for area businesses who are looking for a meeting site. It is likely that the Business Association will move its meetings to the facility. Construction is scheduled to begin late this summer.

New factory coming to Springfield

ACME Widget Corporation announced earlier this month that it will be building a new factory in eastern Springfield, providing around 300 new jobs and a boost to the area's economy.

Nominations sought for offices

The annual elections of the Springfield Business Association are scheduled for August 30. If you are interested in running for office or would like to nominate someone, send notice in writing to the association office before July 10. Open offices are president, vice-president, secretary and treasurer. All members are eligible to run and vote.

Springfield Superstars

Davis receives national award

Henry Davis, president of Davis Printing Services, was recently named Entrepreneur of the Year by the Regional Small Business Leadership Association. Davis, a past president of the Springfield Business Association, balances his time between his business and a variety of volunteer organizations. The printing company is a true family business; Henry's wife and three grown children work there and all play an integral role in making sure things run smoothly.

Davis appreciates the award but is modest about his accomplishments. "A lot of people deserve this more than I do," he says. "I just got lucky. I've got a great family to help me, and I'm filling a need in the Springfield business community."

If you stop in to have some printing done or run into Henry in any of his other pursuits, make sure to offer him your congratulations for this recognition of his achievements.

Yes. Save my spot
at the July 1st
meeting.

Hurry. Your RSVP
must be in by 6/28.

Name _____

Organization _____

Address _____

City, State ZIP _____

Phone ( ) _____

Send right away by:
☐ mail : **Springfield Business Association**, 122 W. Main St., Anytown, US 00000
☐ e-mail : ssb@anytown.org
☐ fax: (555) 555-0301
☐ phone (555) 555-0300

Reply card / RSVP card

Board Members

President:
Martha Birnum
Birnum Communications
555-8258

Vice-President:
Thomas Craddock
Home Hardware
555-2710

Secretary:
Victoria Evans
Springfield Savings Bank
555-4477

Treasurer:
Steven Pauling
Pauling Accounting Services
555-0189

A GOOD ATTITUDE IS IMPORTANT.
FIRST, BUT IT'D BE NICE IF YOU
DID A LITTLE WORK, TOO!

Sidesplitters

When Harvey died, he was given a
choice between Heaven and Hell. He
arranged to tour both before deciding.
Heaven was soft, golden and
peaceful. Hell was filled with wild
parties, loud music and beautiful
women. Harvey chose to go to Hell.

When he arrived, he was thrown to a
fiery pit and forced to work all day
shoveling brimstone. He asked why
everything was so different than it
was on the tour. "That's easy," the
Devil replied; "then you were a
prospect, now you're a customer."

Business School

Make the Internet work for you

The Internet can be an invaluable research tool, but it can also be a huge waste of time. Use these tips to avoid getting stuck in Cyberspace.
• Get on the Net early in the day to avoid high-traffic times
• Upgrade your modem to at least 28.8 bps
• Don't get sidetracked by interesting but irrelevant sites
• Read the "help" files for the search engine you use most often
• Bookmark useful sites for future reference
• If there's reading material you've been meaning to read, glance through it while waiting for large sites to load
• Turn off the graphics capabilities on your browser for really efficient searches
With a little patience and a little common sense, you can make the Internet into an efficient and powerful asset to your business.

For more information on getting online, contact CyberFriends at 555-1234.

How and why to offer fax-on-demand

Whether you have a service- or product-oriented business, a fax-on-demand system can be an easy, efficient way to get information into customers' hands. You can offer catalogs, price lists, brochures or other information on the systems and then publicize the phone number to customers.

There are two different types: For a call-back system, customers phone in an enter the document number and their fax number. The fax-on-demand system calls them back and transmits the document. For a one-call system, callers phone in from their fax machines, enter the document number and hang up. The system then transmits the document to them immediately. One-call systems are cheaper for the sender but will not work for people who use computer faxes.

Regardless of which system you choose, make sure all information is correct and updated frequently. Test the system periodically for speed and accuracy.

For more information on fax-on-demand services, call The Fax Pros at 555-2020.

"In golf, as in life, it's the follow-through that makes the difference."

unknown

Highlights

Annual golf tournament exceeds goals

The Springfield Business Association's golf tournament was a huge success this year. Good publicity and great weather are credited with the turnout for the event, held at Sunfish Lake Resort on May 3. A record number of entries allowed the Association to raise over $3,000 for charity. Thanks to everyone who came and "took a swing at it." Congratulations to the winning foursome: Dave Collins, Marv Johnson, Al Morgan and Tom Drinnen.

Teaser or Announcement

Read on to find out

What sport has been the
subject of the most
Hollywood films?

What's the answer?

(555) 555-0300
Anytown, US 00000
122 W. Main St.
Springfield Business Association

Editor: Susan Anthony
Helping the community grow
BusinessBuzz

Mailing Panel

Why is it upside down?

The mailing panel is flipped upside down on the newsletter design. Automated postal equipment works best when it feeds in your piece on the folded side. To make your newsletter production as easy as possible, this mailing panel is set up in a separate file and designed to be printed, trimmed, flipped and taped to your newsletter.

Marketing with News

In this busy world of marketing, if you're out of sight, you're out of mind.

It's essentially an attention-deficit world out there. You are busy and so are your readers. And, while you have your readers' attention one moment, it's gone the next. That's why paying attention to what I call A-D-D Marketing Methods™ will serve you well.

Here's how it works. Some people read e-mail, some look at faxes, others pay close attention to old-fashioned mail. Some people only *really* pay attention to you when you appear in their peripheral vision—such as being referred by someone else or appearing in the media.

*To plan the timing of each of your news tools, see the timeline form, **catchwav.pdf** on the CD.*

What's a Marketer To Do?

This book is your guide to broadcasting your news to a variety of places. Create a virtual tidal wave of news by using a mixture of methods to reach your targeted audience.

Here's how it works. Let's assume that your goal is to increase attendance at your next event, class or meeting. Use as many of these tools as you can:

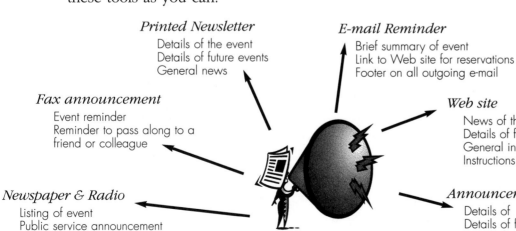

Printed Newsletter
Details of the event
Details of future events
General news

E-mail Reminder
Brief summary of event
Link to Web site for reservations
Footer on all outgoing e-mail

Fax announcement
Event reminder
Reminder to pass along to a
friend or colleague

Web site
News of the coming event
Details of future events
General information about your organization
Instructions for making a reservation

Newspaper & Radio
Listing of event
Public service announcement

Announcements During Event
Details of current event (speaker introduction)
Details of future events
Event information on voice mail recording

Software Tip:

Invest in a contact management program like Outlook, ACT or Goldmine. Spend the time to learn how to use it to reach your target audience with broadcast fax, e-mail and regular mail.

Changing Up

Note the two examples here. You can modify the files with your own logo, change fonts, and add graphics.

See how these all work together? On the other hand, if you only send out an e-mail and link to your Website, you may be *under*-marketing to segments of your target audience.

How to Use This Book

Our goal in the coming pages is to make this process painless. Inside this kit are newsletter, e-mail, postcard, Website and press release formats that you can easily use to reach the people who will make your efforts a success.

The files are designed so that, if you answer the questions in the order that they are asked, you will automatically write in news style. Here's a before and after example using one of the postcard templates:

Your logo **Web***Links*

Subject) tips & trends for (readers) from (organization)   Date/Year

WHAT'S NEW?	FAQS

Subject+ action

Summarize something valuable on your Web site. Why should someone go there?
www.web address.com

Subject+ action

What changes have you made to the site? What have you added or improved?
www.web address.com

Subject+ action

Summarize something valuable on your Web site. Why should someone go there?
www.web address.com

Subject+ action

Summarize something valuable on your Web site. Why should someone go there?
www.web address.com

Name of List

Put a list here: bestsellers, fiction, non-fiction, kids, etc.
1) first book, 2) second book, 3) third book, 4) fourth book, and 5) fifth book.
www.web address.com

Name of List

Put a list here: bestsellers, fiction, non-fiction, kids, etc.
1) first book, 2) second book, 3) third book, 4) fourth book, and 5) fifth book.
www.web address.com

Name of Information

Put information such as store hours, book club meeting times, shipping methods and policies, sale announcements or a customer quote here.

Before. The file called Webcard.pub

Check out the Anytown Library site, www.stacks.com   November 2002

Local Author to Speak

Mary Smith, author of *Here Not There*, will speak at the Anytown Library next month. RSVP and reserve Mary's book (no waiting in line!).
www.stacks.com/RSVP

Sign Up & Save

Add your name to our e-mail newsletter mailing list and get a free bookmark next time you stop by.
www.stacks.com/newsletter

Jane Eyre on Club List

The winter selection for our online book club is *Jane Eyre* by Charlotte Bronte. Sign up now.
www.stacks.com/club.html

December is Dessert Month

See the special selection of cookbooks we have on display.
www.stacks.com/food.html

Librarian Reviews Posted

We've added librarian reviews, so come in and check out Jim, Meghan, and Dave's opinions.
www.stacks.com/readers.html

Books from Anywhere

The Anytown Library is part of the inter-library loan network. Search libraries from across the country for that hard to find title.
www.stacks.com/search

FAQs

What You're Reading

The top 5 most read books are:
1) *Ulysses* 2) *The Catcher in the Rye* 3) *Beloved* 4) *Lolita* and 5) *1984*. See reader reviews at www.stacks.com

Hot Topics at the Library Today

1) Diet, 2) exercise, 3) small business, 4) biography and 5) travel.

After. A postcard for a library that draws traffic to its Web site.

Let's get your news program started by setting a quick plan and selecting the news tools that will best meet your objectives.

Pain-Free Planning

estimated time: 20 minutes

A clear sense of purpose breaks through the fog to your readers' radar. It shows up in your newsletter's name, headlines, content and design. It makes every decision you make when putting together a newsletter EASY.

What to Expect From Your News Program

If you follow the designs and content suggestions in this book and send your news out regularly, you will see the following results based on your type of publication or broadcast (check the results you want).

marketing/sales
- ❑ stay on the minds of customers, prospects and vendors
- ❑ increase sales to current customers
- ❑ increase referrals from customers and vendors
- ❑ shorten time to close sales with prospects
- ❑ reinforce brand identity in your target market

association
- ❑ maximize event attendance
- ❑ retain current members and recruit new members
- ❑ keep members involved
- ❑ lobby for association member interests
- ❑ generate income through ad sales or sponsorship

non-profits
- ❑ increase donations from current donors
- ❑ clarify needs and demonstrate success
- ❑ promote the cause to politicians, media, volunteers
- ❑ partner with other organizations and businesses
- ❑ establish and communicate the organization's cause

internal
- ❑ boost motivation, pride and teamwork from employees
- ❑ increase productivity through education
- ❑ retain and recruit good workers
- ❑ improve quality
- ❑ increase safety awareness

community
- ❑ build sense of community
- ❑ keep people involved and recruit volunteers
- ❑ teach kids about journalism
- ❑ increase meeting attendance
- ❑ build support for local issues

IN THIS CHAPTER:
- ➤ Learn what to expect from your newsletter
- ➤ Create your news strategy and plan
- ➤ Select the news tools to use

Already Have a Plan?

Skip to page 14 and choose your newsletter style.

"And isn't it time we replaced the worn-out, meaningless clichés in our mission statement with some dazzlingly new meaningless clichés?"

Power of Newsletters

❏ Serves as a follow-up to trigger readers' memory of other projects you're working on.

❏ Educates through news.

❏ Keeps everyone updated on changes in your organization.

❏ Reinforces your market commitment.

❏ Unifies a community of readers.

*This form is **quiz.pdf** on the CD.*

Take This Quiz Before You Start

The *Quick and Easy* system makes doing a newsletter as painless as possible. But it does take some time. Take this quiz first:

1. Do you have a mailing list set up or a way to distribute your newsletter to the readers you want to reach?

   ❏ no = set up database and return
   ❏ yes = continue quiz

2. Are you starting this newsletter as a way to generate quick results or is it a long-term marketing and communications tool?

   _____ ❏ quick results = 0 points
   _____ ❏ long-term = 2 points

3. Is your organization changing quickly?

   _____ ❏ no = 0 points
   _____ ❏ yes = 3 points

4. Is educating your readers on your technology, product or services an important part of your marketing?

   _____ ❏ no = 0 points
   _____ ❏ yes = 3 points

5. Are you in a market where it's considered unprofessional to advertise (e.g. legal, medical, professional service, consultant)?

   _____ ❏ no = 0 points
   _____ ❏ yes = 3 points

6. Do you have a variety of different projects, products or services of which you're trying to keep your readers informed?

   _____ ❏ no = 0 points
   _____ ❏ yes = 3 points

7. Do you have access to information that can help your readers make better decisions, improve lives, make money?

   _____ ❏ no = 0 points
   _____ ❏ yes = 3 points

8. Have you ever heard someone say regarding your organization, "I didn't know that you did that."

   _____ ❏ no = 0 points
   _____ ❏ yes = 5 points

   _____ **Total points**

0 to 8 points: Try direct mail, telemarketing or direct selling instead.

9 to 14 points: Proceed. Pay special attention to minimizing costs.

15 to 22 points: You needed a newsletter YESTERDAY. Let's get going.

Create Your Plan by Answering These Questions

Every newsletter has a mission—its purpose and scope both for the reader and for the sponsoring organization. Define your mission by writing it out using the following questions as prompts.

Part 1: About You

This 3-page form is **balance.pdf** *and* **balance.doc** *on the CD.*

1. What is the mission of our organization?

_____

_____

_____

2. What are we known for in the eyes of the outside world?

_____

_____

_____

3. What results do I want (refer to the list on page 7)?

_____

_____

_____

4. What do I want to write about?
   - ❏ my product news
   - ❏ our new cause or fund drive
   - ❏ volunteer jobs available
   - ❏ calendar, meeting and event dates
   - ❏ readership survey
   - ❏ ads telling how to buy specific products
   - ❏ reports of successful past events
   - ❏ speeches I'm giving/ have given
   - ❏ new employees
   - ❏ new clients
   - ❏ new products or services
   - ❏ customer testimonials
   - ❏ letter from the president
   - ❏ letters from customers
   - ❏ new equipment
   - ❏ new facilities
   - ❏ changes to our organization
   - ❏ policy changes
   - ❏ publicity our organization has received
   - ❏ online resources that are available
   - ❏ other:
   - ❏ other:

If You Need Help

If your newsletter is for customers and you don't know the answers to these questions, call one of your top salespeople, fund raisers or membership chairs. In a few minutes, they'll give you a fast start.

Where This is All Headed?

The answers to these questions lead to:

➤ newsletter name
➤ tagline
➤ content
➤ reply card offers
➤ template and layout
➤ distribution methods

*This 3-page form is **balance.pdf** and **balance.doc** on the CD.*

Part 2: About Your Readers

1. Who is the reader we are most trying to serve?

_____

_____

Be very clear here. A newsletter sent to customers may also be sent to employees. Who will you serve first? A vague answer creates a vague newsletter. Trying to serve too many audiences short-changes everyone.

2. Where are they located?

_____

_____

3. What are their average ages? (Use for deciding writing style.)

_____

4. What delivery method do these readers prefer?
   ❑ mail   ❑ e-mail   ❑ fax   ❑ online   ❑ other:

5. What subjects do these people want to read about?
   ❑ issues affecting them
   ❑ industry summaries that save time reading all publications
   ❑ stories of how other people worked with our organization
   ❑ recognition of customers or supporters
   ❑ recognition of members, donors, employees
   ❑ common questions asked by other readers
   ❑ predictions of trends and insider tips
   ❑ opinions and forecasts
   ❑ calendar, meeting and event dates
   ❑ contests and drawings
   ❑ stories, jokes, funny anecdotes, cartoons
   ❑ inspirational quotations
   ❑ facts and trivia
   ❑ news of interesting people
   ❑ customer testimonials
   ❑ book summaries (summarize key points)
   ❑ worksheets and educational information
   ❑ research and statistics
   ❑ customers who've been in the news
   ❑ special offerings, coupons closeouts or remainders
   ❑ free reports, reprints, evaluations, consultations, seminars
   ❑ t-shirt, mugs, caps giveaway
   ❑ company benefits
   ❑ classified ads
   ❑ other resources available online
   ❑ other:

This 3-page form is **balance.pdf** *and* **balance.doc** *on the CD.*

Balancing Content Worksheet

Your newsletter content must strike a balance between what readers want to read and what you want to write about. List your ideas in the two columns below.

NEWS
WHAT READERS WANT TO READ

PROMO
WHAT YOU WANT TO WRITE ABOUT

_____	_____
_____	_____
_____	_____
_____	_____
_____	_____
_____	_____
_____	_____
_____	_____
_____	_____
_____	_____
_____	_____
_____	_____
_____	_____
_____	_____

What is the subject of our newsletter: _____

_____

Who's in Charge?

While you're planning, also find out who has the final approval on newsletter content and final approval on each issue's writing and layout. A part of your mission statement crucial to the happiness of any editor is setting in stone who has the power to approve.

Setting Your Frequency and Budget

How often you should sent out news depends on the answers to these two questions:

1. How often do you need to reach your readers so they won't forget about you?

2. How much time and money do you want to devote to this project?

Your newsletter needs to be published at least quarterly (four times per year) for you to gain the benefits you want. Monthly is best but may be too expensive if you're sending it by mail. Set your budget by using the form on the next page. If you need help determining which size of newsletter to publish, select your newsletter design in the following section, then return to the budgeting worksheet.

11 Best Ways to Save Money on Newsletters

Congratulations! By using this book, you've already completed the first six ways to save money on newsletters.

1. Send a shorter newsletter.
2. Do the writing yourself.
3. Design a postcard newsletter.
4. Do the layout yourself.
5. Design your newsletter for self-mailing (not in an envelope).
6. Send newsletters by e-mail or fax, or publish online.

Now, try these:

7. Use your printer's leftover paper. Printers are happy to get rid of it and readers will probably not know or mind.

8. Reduce the number of names on your list by sending your list to a mailing service that will update all addresses. It's expensive to mail to old lists because most of the addresses have changed.

9. Mail via bulk rate instead of first class. Or, pre-sort and bar code your first class mailings. Find a mailing service who can do this for you. They usually print on less expensive labels (or directly onto the newsletter), saving you the cost of labels.

10. Handout your newsletter instead of mailing.

11. Mail the newsletter only to your most active customers and supporters on your list.

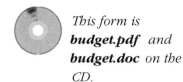

This form is **budget.pdf** *and* **budget.doc** *on the CD.*

Budgeting Worksheet

1st Choice:	Size:	Paper:	Qty:	# Issues/Yr.:	Other:
2nd Choice:	Size:	Paper:	Qty:	# Issues/Yr.:	Other:
3rd Choice:	Size:	Paper:	Qty:	# Issues/Yr.:	Other:

Description	**Cost/Issue** *1st Choice*	**Cost/Issue** *2nd Choice*	**Cost/Issue** *3rd Choice*
Editing, Proofreading			
Paper			
Printing			
Mailing List Printing			
Labeling & Sorting			
Postage			
Other Expenses: Address labels Envelopes Long distance fees for faxes Web & e-mail service fees Web hosting fees			
Total:			
Total Cost/Year: (Total x # Issues/Yr.)			

Start with the size, paper type, quantity for each printing and number of issues you'd like to mail per year. List these specifications under "1st Choice" above. Collect prices for this choice and list them in the first column. If the cost is to high, go back under 2nd choice and change the specifications.

If your project is too expensive, see the previous page for ideas for saving money on newsletters. Also, see the section on e-mail newsletters on page 89 and postcard newsletters on page 85.

*When considering fax, e-mail and Web site news, use the planning form, **newmedia.pdf** shown on page 90.*

Choose Your Design: Fast Formats for Your News

Your choice of design template is based on a combination of what type of publication you want to send with what type of publication your targeted audience wants to read.

Printed Newsletters:

These templates are good if the majority of your list are active clients. The letter-style newsletter gives a warm and personal image. It can be printed right onto your letterhead or on other attractive pre-printed papers.

front: *back:*

 letter.doc, .wpd, .wps

MOST POPULAR:

The two-column format is fast to produce and includes an area for the mailing address to avoid having to use envelopes.

front: *back:*

2c-lettr.doc, .wpd, .wps

The two-column legal format gives you a great newsletter look, lots of room for stories and a skimmable format.

front: *back:*

14

2c-legal.doc, .wpd, .wps

front: *back:*

The three-column format gives you a great newsletter look in a skimmable format. The legal size holds more news and looks professional.
Note: Not available for WordPerfect or Works.

3c-lettr.doc / **3c-legal** (shown here)

front: *back:*

The three-column news format holds the most information of any of the formats but, due to the increased amount of text, it may take longer than an after-noon to put together. This file is set up as a four-page newsletter but can be expand-ed to as many pages as needed or shrunk to one or two pages.

4-pager.doc, .wpd, .wps

If you want feedback from your readers such as RSVPs or requests for more information, use one of the letter-sized designs and tape (the old-fash-ioned way) a reply panel to the bottom to create a legal-sized page.

reply.doc, .wpd, .wps   **rsvp**.doc, .wpd, .wps

Because the mailing area has to be printed upside down to meet postal regulations, this is a separate file to print and flip and tape to the page (the old fashioned way).

mailpanl1.doc, .wpd, .wps   **mailpnl2**.doc, .wpd, .wps

Why are the reply card and mailing panel separate files?

The mail panel, reply and RSVP cards are set up as separate files to allow you the most flexibility possible. They can be added—the old-fashioned way with scissors and tape or glue—to any of the letter- or legal-size designs

Postcard Newsletters (require MS-Publisher):

The small postcard file is perfect when you have three or four news items to get out. It also mails for just 20¢—and the postal service will return address corrections at no charge.

Name*Plate*

(Subject) tips & trends for (readers) from (organization)   Date/Year

WHAT'S NEW?

Subject of news + action created
What is the most important thing that has happened since the last newsletter or will happen soon? What do readers need to know about it? What changes will it cause? Why did it happen?
Who is affected by the story? Who caused it to happen? How will it benefit them? Where did it or will it happen? When did it or will it happen?
Tell readers who to call for more information or what action to take.

Subject of news + action created
What else is important? What do readers need to know about it? What changes will it cause? What is being said about it? Why is it important to readers? Why did it happen? Who is affected by the story? Who

caused it to happen? How will it affect you or your readers? How will it benefit them? How did it happen? Where did it or will it happen? When did it or will it happen?
Tell readers who to call for more information or what action to take.

WHAT DO YOU KNOW?

How to + (action) + (subject)
What should readers know? What should they do? What is your connection to this issue or information? What are some facts and opinions that affect readers about this issue? Why should readers act on this issue or piece of information? When can it be used? Who does it affect?
Tell readers who to call for more information or what action to take.

 smcardft.pub, .doc

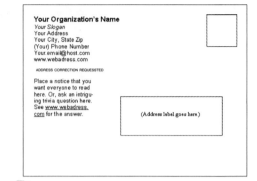

Your Organization's Name
Your Slogan
Your Address
Your City, State Zip
(Your) Phone Number
Your.email@host.com
www.webadress.com

ADDRESS CORRECTION REQUESSTED

Place a notice that you want everyone to read here. Or, ask an intriguing trivia question here. See www.webadress. com for the answer.

(Address label goes here.)

 **smcardbk**.pub, .doc

---

These two postcards are great for drawing readers to articles posted on your Web site or a Web site newsletter. They are set up to mail at 20¢ each. Use **smcardbk** for the reverse side of either card.

Web*Links*

(Subject) tips & trends for (readers) from (organization)   Date/Year

| **WHAT'S NEW?** | **FAQs** |

Subject+ action
Summarize something valuable on your Web site. Why should someone go there?
www.webaddress.com

Subject+ action
What changes have you made to the site? What have you added or improved?
www.webaddress.com

Subject+ action
Summarize something valuable on your Web site. Why should someone go there?
www.webaddress.com

Subject+ action
Summarize something valuable on your Web site. Why should someone go there?
www.webaddress.com

Name of List
Put a list here: bestsellers, fiction, non-fiction, kids, etc.
1) first book, 2) second book, 3) third book, 4) fourth book, and 5) fifth book.
www.webaddress.com

Name of List
Put a list here: bestsellers, fiction, non-fiction, kids, etc.
1) first book, 2) second book, 3) third book, 4) fourth book, and 5) fifth book.
www.webaddress.com

Name of Information
Put information such as store hours, book club meeting times, shipping methods and policies, sale announcements or a customer quote here.

 webcard.pub

Your newsletter is ready...

Go to www.yoursite.com/newsletter issue to see the latest edition of <newsletter name>. In this issue:
> benefit of first article
> benefit of second article
< benefit of third article

Plus the regular features you enjoy:
> standard article
> standard article
> standard article

Visit the site before <deadline> and sign up to receive a free <incentive>. As always, you can read through our back issues here, too, by clicking on <button name>. See you online!

 rdyonWeb.pub

The larger postcards mail at the current first class rate of 34¢ or you could use a bulk mailing service to mail for less. Five to six news items will fit on the card. If you have events to announce, this card works well when the event notices are printed on the back (use **lgcalbk** shown at the bottom of the next page).

(Subject) Tips & Trends for (Readers) from (Customers)   Date/Year

Name*Plate*

WHAT'S NEW?

Subject of news + action created
What is the most important thing that has happened since the last newsletter or will happen soon? What do readers need to know about it? What does it involve? What changes will it cause? What is being said about it? Why is it important to readers? Why did it happen?
Who is affected by the story? Who caused it to happen? How will it affect you or your readers? How will it benefit them? How did it happen? Where did it or will it happen? When did it or will it happen?
Tell readers who to call for more information or what action to take.

Subject of news + action created
What is the most important thing that has happened since the last newsletter or will happen soon? What do readers need to know about it? What does it involve? What changes will it cause? What is being said about it? Why is it important to readers? Why did it happen?
Who is affected by the story? Who caused it to happen? How will it affect you or your readers? How will it benefit them? How did it happen? Where did it or will it happen? When did it or will it happen?
Tell readers who to call for more information or what action to take.

WHO'S NEW?

Person in the news + action created
Who is it about? Why is this person being spotlighted? Why is it important to readers? How has he or she made a difference? How do readers know this person? How did the

subject of the story become involved? What is important about this person? What else has he or she done? What is the person's background? What are his or her plans for the future?
When did this person become involved with the story or the organization? Where did the events being written about occur? Where is the person from? Where did he or she attend school or college?

WHAT DO YOU KNOW?

How to + (intended action) + (subject)
What should readers know? What should they do? What is your connection to this issue or information? What do you recommend? What are some facts and opinions about this issue? How does the issue affect readers? How will it change them? How will it benefit them? Why is it important? Why should readers act on this issue or piece of information? When can it be used? Who does it affect?
Tell readers who to call for more information or what action to take.

How to + (intended action) + (subject)
What should readers know? What should they do? What is your connection to this issue or information? What do you recommend? What are some facts and opinions about this issue? How does the issue affect readers? How will it change them? How will it benefit them? Why is it important? Why should readers act on this issue or piece of information? When can it be used? Who does it affect?
Tell readers who to call for more information or what action to take.

 lgcardft.pub

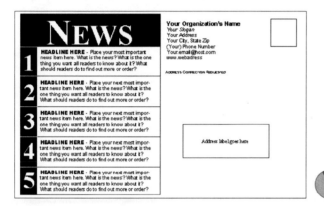

 **lgcalcd**.pub

Organizations that frequently hold events and classes such as associations, museums, schools, libraries and specialty retail stores should consider this card. If you want to include news, print either **lg5news** or **lgnews** (see the next two examples) on the back.

lg5news.pub

An attractive graphic or photo on the front of this card, and the five-news bullets here are the ultimate A-D-D marketing tool! You can be sure that everyone will read your five news items.

lgnewsbk.pub

If you need more space for news items, use this version as the back side of your large postcard.

lgcalbk.pub

This back highlights events and is great when combined with the large postcard containing news, **lgcardft.pub**, from the previous page.

Other News Tools:

Electronic news transmission is a great way to instantly reach readers while stretching your budget. If you're set up to produce some of these high-tech communications, see page 89

Desktop Publishing?

If you plan to use a desktop publishing program such as Quark or Publisher, use this text file to write articles using the content prompts on pages 25 to 64, then, place this text file into your layout.

faxnews..doc, .wpd, .wps

email1.txt

If your mailing list isn't yet updated to include e-mail or fax numbers, use this small postcard to collect information. It mails first class for 20¢.

permissn.pub

Here are several more tools for publicizing your next event.

e-vent.txt

pressrel.doc
(see page 97 for tips)

bookmark.doc

Webnews.htm

Newsworthy Names

estimated time: 15 minutes

The name and tagline for your newsletter is both the billboard and the map for the trip. Your newsletter name includes the name and tagline. At a glance, it tells readers:

❏ the contents of your newsletter
❏ the benefits of reading
❏ whom you've written it for
❏ your organization's name

IN THIS CHAPTER:
➤ Name your newsletter
➤ Type in the tagline and date
➤ Add artwork or logos
➤ Get a little fancy if you feel like it

Regardless of the design you choose, you'll follow the same steps in selecting the name, tagline and dateline for your newsletter. With your computer on in front of you, open the design file that you've chosen from the previous pages (pages 14 through 18).

Name Your Newsletter

The quickest way to name your newsletter is to use your organization's name or the subject covered in your newsletter followed by the word "News" or "Letter."

(Subject) Tips & Trends for *(Readers)* from *(Organization)* page 25	Month or Season/Year

*Name*Plate

Select the word "Name" and type in your organization's name or subject.

(Subject) Tips & Trends for *(Readers)* from *(Organization)* page 25	Month or Season/Year

Retirement News

Select the word "Plate" and type in "News" or "Letter"

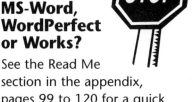

New to MS-Word, WordPerfect or Works?

See the Read Me section in the appendix, pages 99 to 120 for a quick run-through on how the templates work.

Do not keep the name "The Newsletter."

(Subject) Tips & Trends for (Readers) from (Organization) page 25   **Month or Season/Year**

the Carlson **Letter**

You can create a different name by taking the name of your organization or the subject of your newsletter and matching it with one of the News Words starting with the same letter or sound. (See list of News Words on page 120).

(Subject) Tips & Trends for (Readers) from (Organization) page 25   **Month or Season/Year**

Retirement **Riches**

Naming Tip

For a smooth sounding name, use a word that begins with the same letter as your organization's name or newsletter subject.

(Subject) Tips & Trends for (Readers) from (Organization) page 25   **Month or Season/Year**

Carlson **Courier**

You can also have a different type of name all together. (See page 24 for more examples.)

Marketing Tips & Trends for Contractors from the Wizzard of Promotion   **Fall 1999**

Words*from***Woody**

Adding Artwork

If you have your logo as an image on your computer, use it in the nameplate. Or, you can use one of the clip art images provided on the CD (see page 129) or an image from another collection.

To add artwork to your nameplate, insert the cursor after the name of your newsletter. In MS-Word, go to the Insert menu and select Picture. In WordPerfect, go the the Insert menu and select File.

When the clip art or logo is inserted on the screen it may do this:

Or this:

Resize the art by clicking on the boxes in the corners, holding down the Shift key and dragging in or out.

In MS-Publisher

Insert artwork using the Insert menu. Select Picture, then From File.

If you have trouble selecting text near the object, use the Arrange menu to Send to Back or Bring to Front

In MS-Word:

In WordPerfect:

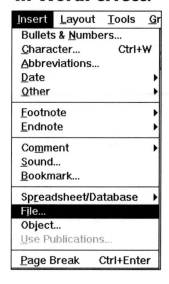

You may also want to make the font size of the newsletter name smaller to fit the clip art.

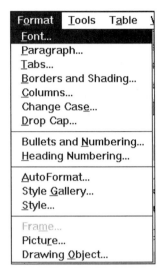

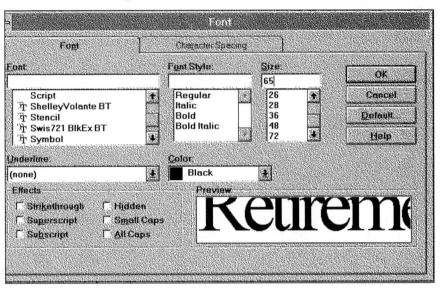

In WordPerfect, you can move the art up or down on the screen using the mouse. In MS-Word you can move the image up or down by going under the Format menu to Font. Click on the tab for Character Spacing. Under Position, select Lowered. Experiment with different numbers—12 point was used here.

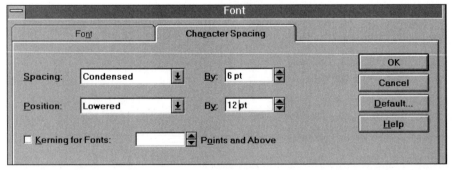

Artwork in nameplate lowered by 12 pt.

Tips for Taglines and Datelines

First, select the area on the top bar with the words, "Month or Season/Year." Type in the date of your newsletter using the month, quarter or season (depending on how often you're going to mail it.

> *monthly:* January 2003
>
> *bi-monthly:* January/February 2003 or Jan./Feb. 2003
>
> *quarterly:* 1st Quarter 2003
>
> *seasonally:* Winter 2003

Not all newsletter names can include benefits. Because you want to communicate the subject and benefit of your newsletter at a glance, include:

- ❑ the intended readers (friends, customers, prospects, sales network, members, employees)

- ❑ the newsletter's content or specialty (if not part of the newsletter name or logo not included)

- ❑ the benefit offered by reading

- ❑ your organization's name (if not part of the newsletter name or logo not included)

Tagline Tip:
Avoid generic taglines such as "A monthly publication of ACME Products" or "The newsletter of ACME."

Set up a tagline that tells readers that the newsletter is just for them.

Type Style Note:

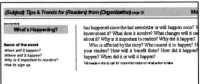

If you backspace after your newsletter name, the type style may shrink and the bars after the nameplate disappear. Select Undo under the Edit menu if this happens.

Note: You don't need your organization's name in the tagline if you've used it as part of the newsletter name or included your logo in the nameplate design.

You can change the tagline formula replacing the words "Tips and Trends" with:

> insights, guide, tips, strategies, trends, tactics, ideas, news, views, hints

Here are some other tagline examples:

> A guide for gardeners from Green Thumb Acres
> Serving motorcycle enthusiasts everywhere
> Focusing on personal finances for the retiree
> News of the world of scuba diving
> Helping you reach your fitness potential
> Proven solutions for real estate success
> Tips, trends and topics for computer users
> Reporting on the world of horses and their riders
> Your connection to the future of telecommunications

Here are some examples of newsletter names along with their taglines:

> Market Ability
> Bottom line strategies for the self-employed

> Money Tips
> Ideas for getting ahead and staying ahead

> Animal Attractions
> Where pets are people too

> Brief Factx
> Tidbits of valuable information for the technical manager

> Subscribe
> Ideas to help gain new subscribers and retain old ones

> Natural News
> From our kitchen to your kitchen

Quick Content

3

estimated time: 90 minutes

N ow it's time to gather your best news—don't worry about exact wording—just type it on the page. We'll polish it up in the next step.

Read the next six pages to get a feel for what mix makes good news, then go the the section that best describes the type of publication you'll be doing: customers, internal, association, non-profit, and community (neighborhood, school, church, club or family).

Content is the key to capturing the attention of your readers while meeting the goals you've set for the newsletter. Through your newsletter's content, you show your readers that you understand their needs and concerns and care enough to address them.

What is Newsworthy?

It's the news element of your newsletter that gets it read. Your newsletter needs a feeling of timeliness—that your news isn't the "olds." Or, your newsletter can summarize and interpret the news, saving your readers time and avoiding information overload.

On the template files, you will create articles based on your answers to these questions that reporters use: who, what, where, why, when and how. The order in which you're asked these questions depends on the subject of your news—whether it's about a person, an event, an education, an offer or straight news.

The newsletter templates guide you through six types of content:

1. **News**—new products, services, causes, events, fund drives, survey results, industry trends, forecasts, news from other sources, privileged insider tips on what's happening in the company, organization, technology or industry

2. **People**—profiles of interesting people, success stories, recognition, welcome messages for new people, employees, clients, members, donors, opinions of what's happening in the industry and predictions of trends, volunteers needed, top members, donors, employees

IN THIS CHAPTER:

➢ Learn about the six types of content

➢ Get ideas for what to write about

➢ Fill your newsletter with news

"Information overload. It's never a pretty sight."

A newsletter should be long enough to say what you need to say and short enough to be read on the way to the wastebasket.

—Mark Beach

25

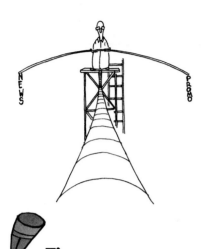

Tip:

Each time you do your newsletter, refer to the mission statement you wrote in Step 1, page 9. Remember to balance your organization's goals with your readers' interests.

3. **Education**—questions and answers, online resources, tips, top 10 reasons, book summaries, motivation, tips for success, editorials, letters, definitions of common terms

4. **Events**— calendars, reminders, deadlines, RSVPs, reports of successful past events

5. **Entertainment**—humor, fun, quotes, trivia, cartoons, jokes, amusing anecdotes, unusual news or stories

6. **Offers**—reply cards, coupons, phone numbers, e-mail addresses, surveys, RSVP numbers, product information online that links to an order form, how to request more information, hours and dates of a special sale

The following illustration shows how the newsletter designs balance out the types of content for you.

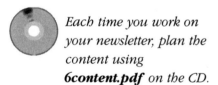

Each time you work on your newsletter, plan the content using **6content.pdf** *on the CD.*

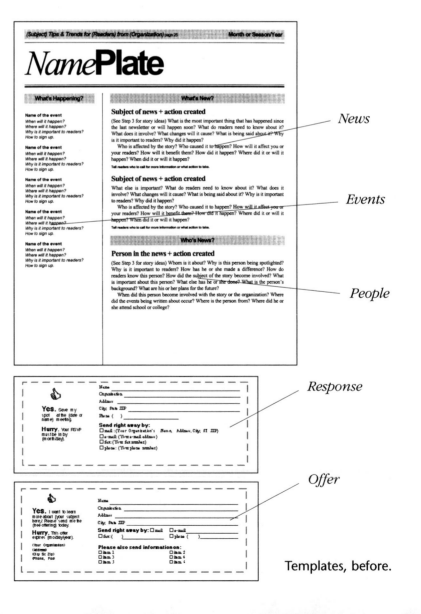

Templates, before.

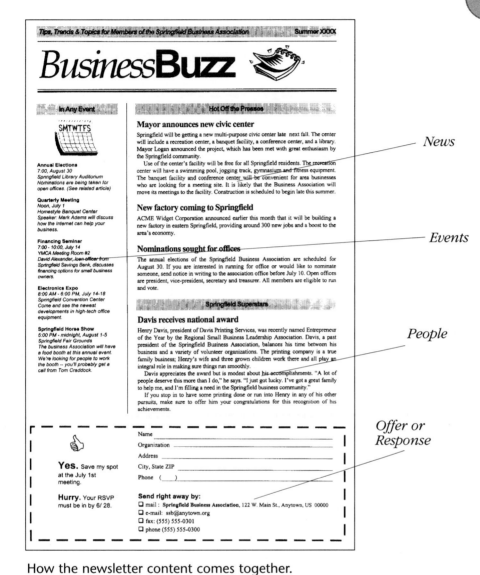

News

Events

People

Offer or Response

How the newsletter content comes together.

*You can also sketch out your newsletter using **fillnews.pdf** on the CD or by using pages 137 and 138 at the end of this book.*

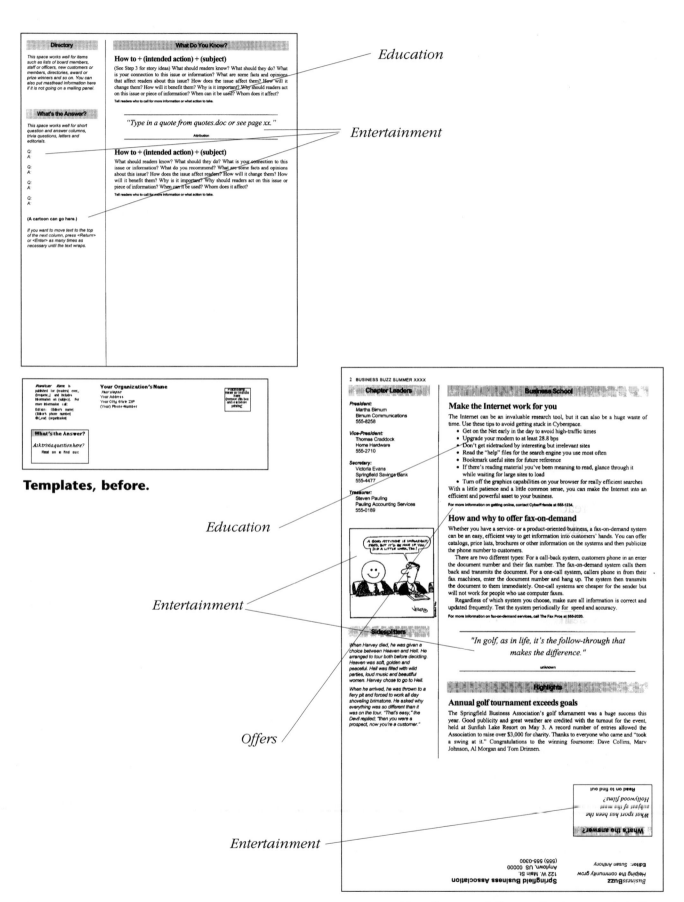

Education

Entertainment

Education

Entertainment

Offers

Entertainment

Templates, before.

How the newsletter content comes together.

You can save time with interviews using **intervw.pdf** *on the CD.*

How to Write at Top Speed

If you are new to news writing, here are a few tips to save you time.

❑ Determine the fastest way to get the information you need. Collect as much as possible by phone or fax or through the mail, including e-mail.

❑ Don't over-research. Collect only what you need and don't get sidetracked by other interesting information.

❑ If an article seems too complicated or research gets too involved, simplify the theme of the article.

❑ Write the rough draft as quickly as possible without fretting over the exact wording.

Note the "Action" Line at the End of Each Brief

Think carefully about what you want readers to do after reading each article. Put this in the action line at the end. Here are some ideas:

❑ summarize your offer

❑ lead readers to the reply card below

❑ mention your guarantees or warranties

❑ give deadlines to offers and other incentives

❑ remind people of follow-up action needed

❑ tell readers to come to the meeting with an RSVP notice

❑ include phone numbers, contact names and reply cards

(Also see ideas for offers on pages 76 and 77.)

You can save time working with reporters using **reporter.pdf** *on the CD.*

Tell readers who to call for more information or what action to take.

This is how the action line appears in the newsletter designs.

New factory coming to Springfield

Acme Widget Corporation announced earlier this month that it will be building a new factory in eastern Springfield, providing around 300 new jobs and a boost to the area's economy. If you've thought about buying a bigger or newer house, this is a great time. The new factory will bring about a better market to sell your existing home, as Acme employees moving into the area will need homes.

Springfield Realty's Relocation Department is working with ACME Widget Corp. to find housing for the new workers. We can help you sell your existing home quickly and easily and make sure you find the perfect home to move into.

If you're thinking about selling, call Mary Garcia at 555-71343.

This is an action line in action.

Communicate with other writers using **submit.pdf** *on the CD.*

Uncopyrightable is the longest English word that doesn't repeat a letter.

Uncopyrightable information is any idea —as long as you don't repeat the words the same way they were originally written.

If you want to reprint copyrighted material, use **cpyright.pdf** *on the CD.*

Brainstorm other sources for your articles using **map-.pdf** *on the CD.*

Quick Lesson in Copyright Law

You're probably starting to wonder about copyrights about now. We all still have the memory of a freshman English teacher ranting and raving about "plagiarism."

While you cannot quote directly from others' material, you can "report" on the information offered. A copyright protects a given combination of words, but does not give any exclusive rights to the information or ideas presented by those words. Industry ethics, however, state that you should list your sources. This also helps readers who want more information on the subject.

Start Filling in Your News

The remainder of this chapter steps you through what to write about in each section of your newsletter. Turn now to the type of newsletter you're writing by looking for the following box at the top of the pages in this chapter:

MARKETING / SALES ☞ page 31

EMPLOYEE / INTERNAL ☞ page 40

ASSOCATION ☞ page 46

NON-PROFIT ☞ page 51

COMMUNITY ☞ page 56

Ideas for Marketing & Sales Newsletters

Use the following questions as idea ticklers. They are designed to help you generate ideas for the different sections in newsletters for customers, prospects and sales network.

News Stories for Sales & Marketing Newsletters

In marketing newsletters, the more you tell about your products and services the better chance you have to sell them. Use the following questions as guidelines.

Keep section heading as is or select the text and change it to one of the options listed on page 126.

Type in a headline or wait until Step 4.

Create your news article by answering these questions directly on the screen(select over the question and type your answer). Use the questions below to get ideas.

What's New?

Subject of news + action created

(See Step 3 for story ideas) What is the most important thing that has happened since the last newsletter or will happen soon? What do readers need to know about it? What does it involve? What changes will it cause? What is being said about it? Why is it important to readers? Why did it happen?

Who is affected by the story? Who caused it to happen? How will it affect you or your readers? How will it benefit them? How did it happen? Where did it or will it happen? When did it or will it happen?

Tell readers who to call for more information or what action to take.

This is how the "News" section appears on the template.

❑ Do you have any new products?

❑ Are you offering any new or additional services?

❑ Do you have any equipment that gives you added capabilities?

❑ What do you offer or do that no other similar organization does?

❑ Have you changed or upgraded any of your products/services?

❑ Why have you made changes to your organization and how will these changes benefit your customers, members or supporters?

❑ Are there any trends you see taking place in your industry? Who is involved in these trends? What changes are they making?

❑ Are you advocating any changes in your industry that will help your clients? What are they?

❑ Has your company been written about in the news recently? Which publication? What did you say? What was the feedback from the article?

❑ How are you helping your customers with these changes you see coming?

Plan the content of each new issue using the form 6content.pdf on the CD.

Ideas for Your News Section

After creating the list, number ideas by priority.

_____

_____

_____

_____

_____

_____

_____

❑ What advice do you have for both your customers and prospects on preparing for the future?

❑ What do you overhear as a part of your day-to-day business?

❑ Have you come across any interesting research or statistics?

❑ From keeping up on your industry, do you see trends developing? What are they? Where do you think your industry will be one year from now? What about five years from now?

❑ Has your product or service been tested against any of your competitors recently? How did it fare?

❑ What new products or services is your company offering?

❑ What have you received the most phone calls about in the last week/month/quarter?

❑ If you were writing a TV ad for your organization, what would it say?

❑ What's the first thing you tell your spouse about when you go home?

❑ How would you describe your job to an 8-year-old?

❑ If you took your children to work with you, what would you show them first?

❑ What is the biggest problem you or your organization have solved lately? How?

❑ What the biggest change you've seen in your field in the past year? What caused it?

❑ What changes do you see occurring in your area of interest in the next five years?

Around Town

New subdivision opens off Highway 100

If you're tired of the long commute downtown and are looking for a new home at a fantastic price, Westwood Glen is the perfect answer. Springfield Realty is developing 80 homesites in the new subdivision with five different models. It's an easy drive from anywhere in the city, but because of the tree-lined perimeter and proximity to two parks, Westwood Glen retains a private, country atmosphere.

Sales manager Dave Edmond says he's never seen so much excitement about a subdivision before it opens. "Buyers are already picking out lots," he said. "Obviously, this location has a lot of appeal."

To see the appeal of Westwood Glen for yourself, stop by between 8 and 5 any day. We are located just west of Grant Road off Highway 100. Act before April 1 to take advantage of Grand Opening Specials.

Call 555-2222 for more information.

A completed "News" section from a real estate marketing newsletter.

People Stories for Sales & Marketing Newsletters

The "People" section can include profiles, success stories, recognition, welcome messages or letters.

Keep section heading as is or select the text and change it to one of the options listed on page 126.

Type in a headline or wait until Step 4.

Create your news article by answering these questions directly on the screen(select over the question and type your answer). Use the questions below to get ideas.

Who's News?

Person in the news + action created

(See Step 3 for story ideas) Whom is it about? Why is this person being spotlighted? Why is it important to readers? How has he or she made a difference? How do readers know this person? How did the subject of the story become involved? What is important about this person? What else has he or she done? What is the person's background? What are his or her plans for the future?

When did this person become involved with the story or the organization? Where did the events being written about occur? Where is the person from? Where did he or she attend school or college?

This is how the "People" section appears on the template.

- ❑ What is the #1 concern on the minds of most of your readers right now? Do you have any advice, offers or products that can help? Can you report on what these concerns are as a general trend?

- ❑ Can you get a quote from one of your customers on how your products or services have helped them?

- ❑ What successes have you recently had? What have been your customers' problems and how have you solved them?

- ❑ Have any of your customers been involved in the news recently? What are they doing? How are they expanding?

- ❑ Who are your new clients? Do they mind if you list them in your newsletter?

- ❑ Have you hired any new people?

- ❑ Have you been given any prestigious awards that your customers will find impressive?

- ❑ What's working for some of your clients and why?

- ❑ What great ideas are out there that you can share to help other companies?

- ❑ Who was the most unusual customer you had this month?

- ❑ Describe your ideal customer.

- ❑ How would that customer describe you?

- ❑ What's the first thing people ask when you tell them your job title?

Ideas for Your People Section

After creating the list, number ideas by priority.

_____

_____

_____

_____

_____

_____

_____

_____

❑ What are you most proud of?

❑ What has been the most common subject of letters from customers or suggestion cards?

❑ What is your company doing to make a difference in your community?

❑ Describe the most rewarding work day of the past month/quarter/year.

Success Stories

Cross-country move causes calamity

Tom and Carol Lawson had known for nine months that they'd be moving their family to Springfield in February. In November, they met Dana Lewis at Springfield Realty, who found them the perfect three-bedroom home near Tom's new workplace.

When moving day arrived, the Lawsons made it safely to Springfield, but their clothes, dishes and furniture didn't. The moving company told them there'd be a shipping delay, but their things should arrive within a week.

When Dana Lewis called to see how they were settling in, Carol told her the whole story. Dana immediately got in touch with a few of Tom and Carol's new neighbors and called a nearby church. Within hours, the Lawsons had enough borrowed and donated dishes and clothes to last until their belongings arrived.

Carol was touched by the experience. "Our first few days here could have been a nightmare, but thanks to Dana and the great Springfield community, it wasn't," she says. "Dana went above and beyond the call of duty. Our experience wasn't the normal way to meet neighbors, but it warmed our hearts more than we can say."

A completed people section from a real estate marketing newsletter.

Education Stories for Sales & Marketing Newsletters

The education section includes helpful articles on subjects related to your company, products or industry. It may also include a message from the president.

If you want to (or must) include a "letter from the president," create (or encourage the president or chairperson to create) a more interesting editorial by listing all of the subjects that are causing irritation or income loss to your readers. What do you know about these issues? What solutions do you have to offer? Do any of these solutions involve use of your products or services?

Another option... make a list of all of the changes affect your industry. What are your predictions for the future? What steps do you

Type in a headline or wait until Step 4.

Keep section heading as is or select the text and change it to one of the options listed on page 127.

Create your news article by answering these questions directly on the screen(select over the question and type your answer). Use the questions below to get ideas.

> ### What Do You Know?
>
> ## How to + (intended action) + (subject)
>
> (See Step 3 for story ideas) What should readers know? What should they do? What is your connection to this issue or information? What are some facts and opinions that affect readers about this issue? How does the issue affect them? How will it change them? How will it benefit them? Why is it important? Why should readers act on this issue or piece of information? When can it be used? Whom does it affect?
>
> **Tell readers who to call for more information or what action to take.**

This is how the "Education" section appears on the template.

think your readers should take to get prepared? Do any of these steps involve your organization?

- ❑ Do you have any questions and answers, quizzes or worksheets that help customers select the right product?

- ❑ What have you recently mentioned to your customers that always spurs their interest?

- ❑ What are the five most common questions your customers ask you?

- ❑ Is there a way you can develop a quiz or self-test that helps customers help themselves?

- ❑ What about your prospects? Do they ask different questions?

- ❑ Do you have advice on how to best use your product or services?

- ❑ What advice do you have for your readers, in general? How can readers thrive in changing times in your industry?

- ❑ What is the background of your products/services? How does knowing it help your customers do business with you?

- ❑ Have you read any good books lately that you can summarize for your readers?

- ❑ How can your readers save money?

- ❑ What are some words that have meanings that are unique to your field such as jargon or buzzwords most people wouldn't know?

- ❑ What do you save the most of for your customers: time? money? worry? something else? How?

- ❑ What are the top five myths people have about your area of interest?

- ❑ See filler stories for Education sections on page 135.

Ideas for Your Education Section

After creating the list, number ideas by priority.

_____

_____

_____

_____

_____

_____

_____

Around the House

Determining your home's condition before you sell

Sellers often wonder how much they should spruce up their homes. The answer depends on the home's age and condition. A well-maintained older home that needs remodeling can be sold it "as is."

A house that has not been well maintained or has any structural flaws needs repairs. A home inspector can help determine your needs. These repairs don't always add value to your home, but you can't sell it without fixing them.

One of the many benefits of using a real estate agent is assistance with questions like these. A Springfield Realty agent will walk through your house with you and discuss areas that need repaired or updated. Your agent will consider these factors when discussing the asking price with you.

Minimize home cooling costs and save energy

As summer approaches, it's time to start thinking about how to cool your home without spending a fortune on air conditioning. Consider the following alternative cooling methods:

- Install an attic fan
- Use ceiling fans in rooms that are used the most
- Switch to a heat pump
- Open deck or patio doors for cross ventilation
- Close off rooms or even floors that are rarely used
- Avoid using the oven during the hottest times of the day

A completed education section from a real estate marketing newsletter.

Events Listings or Stories for Sales & Marketing

Use the sidebar area for your calendar or meeting and event dates.

When designing calendars:

- ❑ give each event a name
- ❑ highlight the name or the date (whichever is more important to readers)
- ❑ print the price of the event or "free"
- ❑ remind readers to call ahead if your events are subject to change
- ❑ consider listing other events around the community to enhance your "community image" (if that's part of your mission)
- ❑ mention if reservations are required and provide the RSVP phone number
- ❑ preview events yet to be scheduled
- ❑ report on successful past events
- ❑ mention top events in more than one place in the newsletter

Questions to consider:

- ❑ Are you speaking at any trade shows or local groups?
- ❑ What trade shows, conventions, special events, seminars are coming up?
- ❑ Are you having any special meetings?
- ❑ Are you holding any customer events?
- ❑ Are you offering any sales or pre-sales?

Keep section heading as is or select the text and change it to one of the options listed on page 127

> **What's Happening?**
>
> **Name of the event**
> *When will it happen?*
> *Where will it happen?*
> *Why is it important to readers?*
> *How to sign up.*
>
> **Name of the event**
> *When will it happen?*
> *Where will it happen?*
> *Why is it important to readers?*
> *How to sign up.*

This is how the "Events" section appears on the template.

Ideas for Your Events Section

After creating the list, number ideas by priority.

_____

_____

_____

_____

_____

_____

_____

_____

> **What's Happening**
>
>
> SMTWTFS
>
> **Buyers Seminar**
> *6:00 - 7:00 pm, March 20*
> *Jefferson High School Gym*
> *Jim Huntley, sales agent for Springfield Realty, will help buyers learn the ins and outs of purchasing a home, including negotiating, financing and buyers agents.*
> *RSVP for a free ticket.*

A completed events section from a real estate marketing newsletter.

37

Ideas for Your Entertainment Section

After creating the list, number ideas by priority.

_____

_____

_____

_____

_____

_____

Entertainment Stories for Sales & Marketing

Capture the attention of every reader with quotes, humor and cartoons.

> _"Type in a quote from quotes.doc or see page xx."_
>
> **Attribution**

This is how the entertainment section appears on the template.

- ❏ What are your favorite quotes?
- ❏ What are the "quotables" in your industry?
- ❏ Do you have any funny (yet tasteful) stories or jokes that relate to your organization?
- ❏ Do you have fun facts about your organization or industry?
- ❏ Include a quote from the CD (see page 131).
- ❏ Include a trivia question from the CD (see page 132).
- ❏ Include a cartoon from the CD (see page 129).

Pop Quiz

Q: When was Springfield founded?

Q: Who was the first Mayor?

Q: What was Springfield's population in 1900?

Q: In what sports have Springfield high school teams won state championships?

A: swimming (1977), field hock wrestling (1995), football (1983), baseball:A

A: 2,157

A: James Douglas Thomas

A: 1887

A completed entertainment section from a real estate marketing newsletter.

News for Home Buyers & Sellers from Springfield Realty　　　　　　Spring xxxx

Homeowners **Hotline**

What's Happening

Buyers Seminar
6:00 - 7:00 pm, March 20
Jefferson High School Gym
Jim Huntley, sales agent for
Springfield Realty, will help buyers
learn the ins and outs of purchasing
a home, including negotiating,
financing and buyers agents.
RSVP for a free ticket.

Open Houses
20117 Highway 85
10:00 am - 3:00 pm, March 20

383 Plymouth Drive
noon - 4:00pm, March 21

15 Elm Drive
noon - 4:00 pm, March 28

Real Estate Class
Springfield Community College
March 10 through April 30
7:00 pm - 9:30 pm, Tues. & Thurs.
Liz Morgan, licensed broker, teaches
the licensing class for new agents.
Fee: $10. Call Fred at the college,
555-9876, to register.

Financing Seminar
Springfield Library.
7:00 pm - 10:00 pm, April 14
David Alexander, loan officer from
Springfield Savings Bank, discusses
financing options for home buyers.
Free.

Home Decorating Tips
Springfield Design & Decor
6:30 pm - 7:30 pm, April 21
Karen Coring, interior designer,
provides tips and trends in home
decorating. Free

Around Town

New subdivision opens off Highway 100

If you're tired of the long commute downtown and are looking for a new home at a fantastic price, Westwood Glen is the perfect answer. Springfield Realty is developing 80 homesites in the new subdivision with five different models. It's an easy drive from anywhere in the city, but because of the tree-lined perimeter and proximity to two parks, Westwood Glen retains a private, country atmosphere.

Sales manager Dave Edmond says he's never seen so much excitement about a subdivision before it opens. "Buyers are already picking out lots," he said. "Obviously, this location has a lot of appeal."

To see the appeal of Westwood Glen for yourself, stop by between 8 and 5 any day. We are located just west of Grant Road off Highway 100. Act before April 1 to take advantage of Grand Opening Specials.

Call 555-2222 for more information.

New factory coming to Springfield

Acme Widget Corporation announced earlier this month that it will be building a new factory in eastern Springfield, providing around 300 new jobs and a boost to the area's economy. If you've thought about buying a bigger or newer house, this is a great time. The new factory will bring about a better market to sell your existing home, as Acme employees moving into the area will need homes.

Springfield Realty's Relocation Department is working with ACME Widget Corp. to find housing for the new workers. We can help you sell your existing home quickly and easily and make sure you find the perfect home to move into.

If you're thinking about selling, call Mary Garcia at 555-71343.

Star Performers

Debbie Maxwell named Agent of the Year

If you spend much time driving around Springfield, you've probably seen Debbie Maxwell's name on a lot of "Sold" signs. She was the top-selling agent at Springfield Realty last year and was named Agent of the Year. She credits her enthusiasm and concern for people as the biggest factors in her success. "I really love my job," she said. "It's so satisfying to match up the perfect buyer with the perfect home."

When not playing matchmaker for buyers and sellers, Debbie stays busy as the mom of Jason (2 years old) and Tiffany (5 years old) and wife of Steve (who won't tell his age). Debbie invites anyone who has thought about buying or selling a home to give her a call at 555-2100 and take advantage of her knowledge and experience. She says, "If you've been thinking your back yard is too small or you'd love to be closer to your kids' school, let me help make your dreams come true."

Pop Quiz

Q: When was Springfield founded?

Q: Who was the first Mayor?

Q: What was Springfield's
population in 1900?

Q: In what sports have Springfield
high school teams won state
championships?

*A: baseball (1983), football
wrestling (1995), field hock-
swimming (1977)*

A: 2,157

A: James Douglas Thomas

A: 1887

Laugh Tracks

Q: If a red house is made of red
wood and a blue house is made of
blue wood, what is a green house
made of?

A: Glass!

Thanks to Sarah Morris, 10 years old

Around the House

Determining your home's condition before you sell

Sellers often wonder how much they should spruce up their homes. The answer depends on the home's age and condition. A well-maintained older home that needs remodeling can be sold "as is."

A house that has not been well maintained or has any structural flaws needs repairs. A home inspector can help determine your needs. These repairs don't always add value to your home, but you can't sell it without fixing them.

One of the many benefits of using a real estate agent is assistance with questions like these. A Springfield Realty agent will walk through your house with you and discuss areas that need repaired or updated. Your agent will consider these factors when discussing the asking price with you.

Minimize home cooling costs and save energy

As summer approaches, it's time to start thinking about how to cool your home without spending a fortune on air conditioning. Consider the following alternative cooling methods:
- Install an attic fan
- Use ceiling fans in rooms that are used the most
- Switch to a heat pump
- Open deck or patio doors for cross ventilation
- Close off rooms or even floors that are rarely used
- Avoid using the oven during the hottest times of the day

*"Where we love is home, home that our feet may
leave, but not our hearts."*

Justice Oliver Wendell Homes

Success Stories

Cross-country move causes calamity

Tom and Carol Lawson had known for nine months that they'd be moving their family to Springfield in February. In November, they met Dana Lewis at Springfield Realty, who found them the perfect three-bedroom home near Tom's new workplace.

When moving day arrived, the Lawsons made it safely to Springfield, but their clothes, dishes and furniture didn't. The moving company told them there'd be a shipping delay, but their things should arrive within a week.

When Dana Lewis called to see how they were settling in, Carol told her the whole story. Dana immediately got in touch with a few of Tom and Carol's new neighbors and called a nearby church. Within hours, the Lawsons had enough borrowed and donated dishes and clothes to last until their belongings arrived.

Carol was touched by the experience. "Our first few days here could have been a nightmare, but thanks to Dana and the great Springfield community, it wasn't," she says. "Dana went above and beyond the call of duty. Our experience wasn't the normal way to meet neighbors, but it warmed our hearts more than we can say."

Ideas for Offers
(see page 29)

After creating the list,
number ideas by priority.

_____

_____

_____

_____

_____

_____

_____

A completed marketing-style
newsletter from a real estate
company.

*Plan the content of each new issue using the form **6content.pdf** on the CD.*

Ideas for Employee Newsletters

The employee publication is a balance of information with entertainment. You must please management by running the information it wants to see in print and you must please the employees by providing information they want to read.

The book *Public Relations: The Profession and the Practice* (written by Otis Baskin and Craig Aronoff) says to include:

- ❏ 50 percent information about the organization (local, national, and international)
- ❏ 20 percent employee information (benefits, quality of working life, etc.)
- ❏ 20 percent relevant noncompany information (competitors, community, etc.)
- ❏ 10 percent humor, motivation, small talk and personals

News Stories

Employees want to know about the company's products and services as well as industry news. Use the following questions as guidelines.

- ❏ What has been the most common subject of letters from customers or suggestion cards?
- ❏ What is your company doing to make a difference in your community?
- ❏ Are any unusual problem-solving techniques being used in your company?

Type in a headline or wait until Step 4.

Keep section heading as is or select the text and change it to one of the options listed on page 126.

Create your news article by answering these questions directly on the screen(select over the question and type your answer). Use the questions below to get ideas.

What's New?

Subject of news + action created

(See Step 3 for story ideas) What is the most important thing that has happened since the last newsletter or will happen soon? What do readers need to know about it? What does it involve? What changes will it cause? What is being said about it? Why is it important to readers? Why did it happen?

Who is affected by the story? Who caused it to happen? How will it affect you or your readers? How will it benefit them? How did it happen? Where did it or will it happen? When did it or will it happen?

Tell readers who to call for more information or what action to take.

This is how the "News" section appears on the template.

❑ What have you received the most phone calls about in the last week/month/quarter?

❑ Who was the most unusual customer you had this month?

❑ What new legal issues may affect your company or your business?

❑ Has your field been featured in any movies or TV shows? How was it portrayed? How accurate was the portrayal?

❑ What is your company doing to help the environment (recycling, waste reduction, etc.)?

❑ List any job, position, or committee openings in your organization that could be filled internally.

Ideas for Your News Section

After creating the list, number ideas by priority.

_____

_____

_____

_____

_____

_____

_____

_____

News to Know

New computer system goes online

SSB's new interactive customer information system was introduced on May 17, bringing helpful changes to the way customer accounts are entered and tracked. The new system, called CREST (Customer Records Entry Setup and Tracking), is a state-of-the-art network allowing fast and efficient communication between branches. Complete customer information will now be immediately available on the screen, eliminating time-consuming phone calls from one branch to another.

SSB has scheduled training dates to help employees make a smooth transition to the new system. Dates are posted around the branches. Check with your supervisor for scheduling. The designers of CREST are from the Computer Programming and Operations Department. They are certain that once SSB employees are used to the new system, they will be thrilled with its speed and the depth of information.

For further information, call Chris in Computer Programming at extension 123.

A completed "News" section from an employee newsletter.

People Stories for Employee Newsletters

The "People" section can include employee pro-files, success stories, employee news and awards.

Keep section heading as is or select the text and change it to one of the options listed on page 126.

Type in a headline or wait until Step 4.

Create your news article by answering these questions directly on the screen(select over the question and type your answer). Use the questions below to get ideas.

Who's News?

Person in the news + action created

(See Step 3 for story ideas) Whom is it about? Why is this person being spotlighted? Why is it important to readers? How has he or she made a difference? How do readers know this person? How did the subject of the story become involved? What is important about this person? What else has he or she done? What is the person's background? What are his or her plans for the future?

    When did this person become involved with the story or the organization? Where did the events being written about occur? Where is the person from? Where did he or she attend school or college?

This is how the "People" section appears on the template.

Ideas for Your People Section

After creating the list, number ideas by priority.

❑ What awards, recognition or commendations have been received in the past month/quarter/year?

❑ What department or division has stood out recently in terms of high quality or few mistakes or few complaints?

❑ Who is a "behind the scenes" or "unsung hero"?

❑ Profile someone who has an unusual hobby or interest outside of work.

❑ What's been the biggest topic of discussion in the employee lounge?

❑ List employee birthdays, weddings, births of children, work-place anniversaries.

❑ Ask people how they entered their field. List several answers.

SSB Celebrities

Thompson promoted to Branch Manager

Elizabeth Thompson was named manager of the new Grant Avenue branch, scheduled to open on August 10. Elizabeth has been with SSB for 15 years. She began in customer service, moved up through new accounts and was promoted to

---

A partial "People" articled from an employee newsletter.

Education Stories for Employee Newsletters

The education section includes helpful articles on subjects related to your company, products or industry. It may also include a message from the president (see also page 34).

Keep section heading as is or select the text and change it to one of the options listed on page 127.

Type in a headline or wait until Step 4.

Create your news article by answering these questions directly on the screen(select over the question and type your answer). Use the questions below to get ideas.

What Do You Know?

How to + (intended action) + (subject)

(See Step 3 for story ideas) What should readers know? What should they do? What is your connection to this issue or information? What are some facts and opinions that affect readers about this issue? How does the issue affect them? How will it change them? How will it benefit them? Why is it important? Why should readers act on this issue or piece of information? When can it be used? Whom does it affect?

Tell readers who to call for more information or what action to take.

This is how the "Education" section appears on the template.

❑ What opportunities are coming up for continuing education?

❑ What are some seminars, conferences or workshops employees can or should attend?

❑ Reprint a letter from a customer. If positive, it can stand alone. If negative, explain what went wrong and how the problem was addressed.

❑ What organizations or associations would be beneficial for employees to join?

❑ Ask people what was the last book they read or movie they saw and whether they would recommend it. List several answers.

❑ Include a regular advice column for issues such as dealing with customer complaints or handling conflicts with fellow workers.

❑ What are some words that have meanings that are unique to your field—jargon or buzzwords most people wouldn't know?

❑ Include tips for diet, exercise or general health.

❑ See filler stories for Education sections on page 135.

Ideas for Your Education Section

After creating the list, number ideas by priority.

_____

_____

_____

_____

_____

_____

_____

A completed "Education" section from an employee newsletter.

Bank on It

Improve your telephone persona

We all spend a lot of time on the phone—so much so that it's easy to take for granted. Use these techniques to make sure you maintain a friendly, professional manner when on the phone:

- Answer before the third ring
- Smile when you speak on the phone—it shows in your voice
- State your name when you answer
- Repeat customer questions back to them to make sure you've understood
- Ask customers to call back if they have other questions
- Thank customers for banking with SSB

Keep section heading as is or select the text and change it to one of the options listed on page 127.

Name of the event
When will it happen?
Where will it happen?
Why is it important to readers?
How to sign up.

Name of the event
When will it happen?
Where will it happen?
Why is it important to readers?
How to sign up.

This is how the "Events" section appears on the template.

Ideas for Your Events Section

After creating the list, number ideas by priority.

_____

_____

_____

_____

_____

_____

_____

Event Listing and Stories for Employee Newsletters

(See tips for calendar design on page 37)

❑ What are some upcoming company events?

❑ Deadlines for benefit forms, health plan updates.

❑ Promote sign-ups for blood drives.

❑ Promote sign-ups for organization teams.

Invitations

SMTWTFS

Company Picnic
July 10, noon-5:00 pm
Sunfish Park
Join your co-workers in an afternoon of food, games and fun. Each department will bring a different category of food. Participate in volleyball, badminton, and other games at this annual celebration.
See the sign up sheet in the cafeteria.

A completed "Events" section from an employee newsletter.

Entertainment Stories

❑ Include "Top 10" lists.

❑ What are your favorite quotes?

❑ Who are the "quotables" in your industry?

❑ Do you have any funny (yet tasteful) stories or jokes that relate to your organization?

❑ Do you have any fun facts about your organization or industry?

❑ Include a quote from the CD (see page 131).

❑ Include a trivia question from the CD (see page 132).

❑ Include a cartoon from the CD (see page 129).

Ideas for Your Entertainment Section

After creating the list, number ideas by priority.

_____

_____

_____

_____

_____

_____

_____

A completed employee newsletter from a bank.

Ideas for Offers (see page 29)

After creating the list, number ideas by priority.

_____

_____

_____

_____

_____

_____

_____

_____

Especially for Employees of Springfield Savings Bank   Summer XXXX

SSB **Smalltalk**

Invitations

Company Picnic
July 10, noon-5:00 pm
Sunfish Park
Join your co-workers in an afternoon of food, games and fun. Each department will bring a different category of food. Participate in volleyball, badminton, and other games at this annual celebration.
See the sign up sheet in the cafeteria.

Continuing Education Classes
June 6, 7:30 am -10:00 am
Main Street Branch
Learn more about amortization tables and their effects on mortgage financing.
Sign up by calling 555-3434.

June 20, 7:30 am -10:00 am
Main Street Branch
Learn successful techniques for handling customer complaints.
Sign up by calling 555-3434.

July 7, 5:00 pm - 8:00 pm
South Morgan Branch
Learn how the Internet will change banking into the next century.
Sign up by calling 555-3434.

CPR Training
August 1, noon - 2:00 pm
Main Street Branch
Opportunity to learn life-saving techniques from a certified trainer
Sign up by calling 555-3434.

News to Know

New computer system goes online

SSB's new interactive customer information system was introduced on May 17, bringing helpful changes to the way customer accounts are entered and tracked. The new system, called CREST (Customer Records Entry Setup and Tracking), is a state-of-the-art network allowing fast and efficient communication between branches. Complete customer information will now be immediately available on the screen, eliminating time-consuming phone calls from one branch to another.

SSB has scheduled training dates to help employees make a smooth transition to the new system. Dates are posted around the branches. Check with your supervisor for scheduling. The designers of CREST are from the Computer Programming and Operations Department. They are certain that once SSB employees are used to the new system, they will be thrilled with its speed and the depth of information.

For further information, call Chris in Computer Programming at extension 123.

New factory coming to Springfield

Acme Widget Corporation announced earlier this month that it will be building a new factory in eastern Springfield, providing around 300 new jobs and a boost to the area's economy. SSB is offering special accounts for Acme employees, including no-minimum-balance savings accounts and special rate CD's. Look for Acme packets to arrive in branches by mid-June. Possible referrals include the mortgage department for Acme employees who'll be moving into Springfield.

Debit cards receive great response

When they were introduced last fall, the most common reaction customers had to debit cards was "What is it?" Since SSB was the first bank in the area to offer debit cards, most customers were unfamiliar with them and many were hesitant.

But thanks to a successful ad campaign and knowledgeable training by SSB employees, customer response has become very favorable toward the cards. More customers are using SSB debit cards at ATM machines and point-of-sale locations than any other area bank's cards. You've done a great job promoting the cards and training customers in their use. Keep up the good work!   -- *John Sanders, Pres. SSB*

SSB Celebrities

Thompson promoted to Branch Manager

Elizabeth Thompson was named manager of the new Grant Avenue branch, scheduled to open on August 10. Elizabeth has been with SSB for 15 years. She began in customer service, moved up through new accounts and was promoted to

---

Trivia Teasers

Q: What key is the dial tone of a normal telephone?

Q: How far away can you hear a lion's roar?

Q: What's the average life span of a tastebud?

Q: How many earthquakes does the earth have in a year?

Q: Who are the only two people in the baseball Hall of Fame who had nothing to do with baseball?

A: Abbott and Costello

A: About 50,000

A: 10 days

A: 5 miles

A: The Key of F

Remember to let customers know about the Christmas Club savings account plan.

Thompson Promotion, continued
assistant manager of the Twelfth Avenue branch two years ago. She looks forward to assuming her new responsibilities but says she'll miss working at Twelfth Avenue.

"We're really excited about the new branch. It's a beautiful facility, and SSB will have a strong presence in that part of town," she says. "It will be hard to leave here, though; I will really miss my co-workers and the customers."

Stop by the Grant Avenue branch during the week of August 10 to see the new facility and offer your congratulations to Elizabeth. Tell customers about the new branch and let them know that cake and punch will be available at the branch during that week.

The Grant Ave. branch is located at 554 Grant Ave., 555-3456.

Teller's caring response creates satisfied customer

On March 5, a customer came to Florence Green's teller window (North Axle Street Branch) with a stack of canceled checks and a confused look. The customer explained that her bank statement had just arrived and she didn't know how to read it. Florence checked the customer's information and learned that her husband had passed away the month before. Florence expressed her sympathy and asked if the woman's husband had always taken care of financial matters.

With tears in her eyes, the customer answered that she was lost without her husband and asked for Florence's help in figuring out her balance. Florence started to send her to customer service, but the sad, trusting look in the customer's eyes made her want to help the woman herself. Florence told the customer that her lunch hour would start in fifteen minutes, and if the she could wait, Florence would sit with her during lunch and explain the process.

Florence spent her entire lunch hour with the customer, who left feeling comfortable and secure. This was an outstanding example of going above and beyond the call of duty for excellent customer service.

"If you believe that you can, or if you believe you cannot, you are probably right."

Mark Twain, American author

Bank on It

Improve your telephone persona

We all spend a lot of time on the phone—so much so that it's easy to take for granted. Use these techniques to make sure you maintain a friendly, professional manner when on the phone:

- Answer before the third ring
- Smile when you speak on the phone—it shows in your voice
- State your name when you answer
- Repeat customer questions back to them to make sure you've understood
- Ask customers to call back if they have other questions
- Thank customers for banking with SSB

Whether customers are in front of you or across town, always remember to project a customer-friendly, service-minded attitude. Even when you're busy and customers are waiting, don't underestimate the power of the telephone.

Keep section heading as is or select the text and change it to one of the options listed on page 126.

Type in a headline or wait until Step 4.

Create your news article by answering these questions directly on the screen(select over the question and type your answer). Use the questions below to get ideas.

*Plan the content of each new issue using the form **6content.pdf** on the CD. (See a thumbnail of the form on page 31.)*

Ideas for Your News Section

After creating the list, number ideas by priority.

_____

_____

_____

_____

_____

_____

_____

A completed "News" section from an association newsletter.

News Stories for Association Newsletters

In association newsletters, your "News" section reports on conditions and trends in the industry or group you serve.

What's New?

Subject of news + action created

(See Step 3 for story ideas) What is the most important thing that has happened since the last newsletter or will happen soon? What do readers need to know about it? What does it involve? What changes will it cause? What is being said about it? Why is it important to readers? Why did it happen?

Who is affected by the story? Who caused it to happen? How will it affect you or your readers? How will it benefit them? How did it happen? Where did it or will it happen? When did it or will it happen?

Tell readers who to call for more information or what action to take.

This is how the "News" section appears on the template.

❑ What are some new products that would benefit members?

❑ What are some legal issues that affect your association and what is the association's stand on them?

❑ How has your association changed in the past year? Five years? Over its history?

❑ What changes do you see within your association over the next decade?

❑ What networking opportunities exist within your association?

❑ Has there been any important news in related industries?

❑ What are the benefits of belonging to your association?

❑ What are the biggest problems members face and how can they be corrected or reduced?

❑ Encourage membership renewals, newsletter pass-alongs and recommendations for non-members to join.

❑ What national events or issues directly affect your chapter?

Hot Off the Presses

Mayor announces new civic center

Springfield will be getting a new multi-purpose civic center late next fall. The center will include a recreation area, a banquet facility, a conference center, and a library. Mayor Logan announced the project, which has been met with great enthusiasm by the Springfield community.

Use of the center's facility will be free for all Springfield residents. The recreation center will have a swimming pool, jogging track, gymnasium and fitness equipment. The banquet facility and conference center will be convenient for area businesses who are looking for a meeting site. It is likely that the Business Association will move its meetings to the facility. Construction is scheduled to begin late this summer.

People Stories for Association Newsletters

The "People" section includes member profiles, success stories, recognition of volunteers, welcome messages and other messages or letters.

Keep section heading as is or select the text and change it to one of the options listed on page 126.

Type in a headline or wait until Step 4.

Create your news article by answering these questions directly on the screen(select over the question and type your answer). Use the questions below to get ideas.

Who's News?

Person in the news + action created

(See Step 3 for story ideas) Whom is it about? Why is this person being spotlighted? Why is it important to readers? How has he or she made a difference? How do readers know this person? How did the subject of the story become involved? What is important about this person? What else has he or she done? What is the person's background? What are his or her plans for the future?

When did this person become involved with the story or the organization? Where did the events being written about occur? Where is the person from? Where did he or she attend school or college?

This is how the "People" section appears on the template.

- ❑ Who are some members who stand out? Why? What are their accomplishments?
- ❑ What positions on committees or in offices need to be filled and when?
- ❑ What innovative techniques are being used by members that others would benefit from?
- ❑ What vendors or suppliers work well with your organization?
- ❑ Who within your association deserves thanks or recognition for work done for the association?
- ❑ List new chapter members.

Ideas for Your People Section

After creating the list, number ideas by priority.

_____

_____

_____

_____

_____

_____

_____

_____

Springfield Superstars

Davis receives national award

Henry Davis, president of Davis Printing Services, was recently named Entrepreneur of the Year by the Regional Small Business Leadership Association. Davis, a past president of the Springfield Business Association, balances his time between his business and a variety of volunteer organizations. The printing company is a true family business; Henry's wife and three grown children work there and all play an integral role in making sure things run smoothly.

Davis appreciates the award but is modest about his accomplishments. "A lot of people deserve this more than I do," he says. "I just got lucky. I've got a great family to help me, and I'm filling a need in the Springfield business community."

If you stop in to have some printing done or run into Henry in any of his other pursuits, make sure to offer him your congratulations for this recognition of his achievements.

A completed "People" section from an association newsletter.

Education Stories for Association Newsletters

The "Education" section includes helpful articles on subjects that are interesting to your members. See page 34 for information on including editorials and letters.

Type in a headline or wait until Step 4.

Keep section heading as is or select the text and change it to one of the options listed on page 127.

Create your news article by answering these questions directly on the screen(select over the question and type your answer). Use the questions below to get ideas.

What Do You Know?

How to + (intended action) + (subject)

(See Step 3 for story ideas) What should readers know? What should they do? What is your connection to this issue or information? What are some facts and opinions that affect readers about this issue? How does the issue affect them? How will it change them? How will it benefit them? Why is it important? Why should readers act on this issue or piece of information? When can it be used? Whom does it affect?

Tell readers who to call for more information or what action to take.

This is how the "Education" section appears on the template.

Ideas for Your Education Section

After creating the list, number ideas by priority.

❑ What tips can members provide to benefit other members?

❑ What books or audio tapes should members know about?

❑ What other association publications should readers know about (Web sites, reports, books, magazines)?

❑ What is some jargon used by your association that it may be helpful or fun to define?

❑ What are the most common myths or misconceptions about your industry?

❑ See filler stories for Education sections on page 135.

A completed "Education" section from an association newsletter.

Business School

Make the Internet work for you

The Internet can be an invaluable research tool, but it can also be a huge waste of time. Use these tips to avoid getting stuck in Cyberspace.
- Get on the Net early in the day to avoid high-traffic times
- Upgrade your modem to at least 28.8 bps
- Don't get sidetracked by interesting but irrelevant sites
- Read the "help" files for the search engine you use most often
- Bookmark useful sites for future reference
- If there's reading material you've been meaning to read, glance through it while waiting for large sites to load
- Turn off the graphics capabilities on your browser for really efficient searches

With a little patience and a little common sense, you can make the Internet into an efficient and powerful asset to your business.

For more information on getting online, contact CyberFriends at 555-1234.

Event Listings or Stories for Association Newsletters

The "Events" section lists your own events or other upcoming events in your community. (See tips for calendar designs on page 37.)

❑ What are upcoming events your members would be interested in (meetings, conferences, seminars, workshops)?

❑ Report on past events that members attended.

Entertainment Stories for Association Newsletters

People need a break from the day's pressures. Include an inspirational or amusing quote, cartoon or story anywhere within the newsletter.

❑ Tell a tasteful joke or story you've recently heard.

❑ Include a quote from the CD (see page 131).

❑ Include a trivia question from the CD (see page 132).

❑ Include a cartoon from the CD (see page 129).

Keep section heading as is or select the text and change it to one of the options listed on page 127.

What's Happening?
Name of the event
When will it happen?
Where will it happen?
Why is it important to readers?
How to sign up.
Name of the event
When will it happen?
Where will it happen?
Why is it important to readers?
How to sign up.

This is how the "Events" section appears on the template.

In Any Event

Annual Elections
7:00 pm, August 30
Springfield Library Auditorium
Nominations are being taken for open offices. (See related article)

Quarterly Meeting
Noon, July 1
Homestyle Banquet Center
Speaker: Mark Adams will discuss how the Internet can help your business.
RSVP by using the form below.

Financing Seminar
8:00 am - 10:00 am, July 14
YMCA Meeting Room #2
David Alexander, loan officer from Springfield Savings Bank, discusses financing options for small business owners.
Call 555-3636 for free registration.

A completed "Events" section from an association newsletter.

Ideas for Your Events Section

After creating the list, number ideas by priority.

_____

_____

_____

_____

_____

_____

_____

Ideas for Your Entertainment Section

After creating the list, number ideas by priority.

_____

_____

_____

_____

_____

Ideas for Offers
(see page 29)

After creating the list, number ideas by priority.

_____

_____

_____

_____

_____

A completed "Entertainment" section from an association newsletter.

Tips, Trends & Topics for Members of the Springfield Business Association   Summer XXXX

BusinessBuzz

In Any Event

Annual Elections
7:00 pm, August 30
Springfield Library Auditorium
Nominations are being taken for open offices. (See related article)

Quarterly Meeting
Noon, July 1
Homestyle Banquet Center
Speaker: Mark Adams will discuss how the Internet can help your business.
RSVP by using the form below.

Financing Seminar
8:00 am - 10:00 am, July 14
YMCA Meeting Room #2
David Alexander, loan officer from Springfield Savings Bank, discusses financing options for small business owners.
Call 555-3636 for free registration.

Electronics Expo
8:00 am - 6:00 pm, July 14-18
Springfield Convention Center
Come and see the newest developments in high-tech office equipment.

Springfield Horse Show
5:00 pm - midnight, August 1-5
Springfield Fair Grounds
The business Association will have a food booth at this annual event. We're looking for people to work the booth -- you'll probably get a call from Tom Craddock. Tickets are $5 and are available at the door.

Answer: Boxing

Hot Off the Presses

Mayor announces new civic center

Springfield will be getting a new multi-purpose civic center late next fall. The center will include a recreation area, a banquet facility, a conference center, and a library. Mayor Logan announced the project, which has been met with great enthusiasm by the Springfield community.

Use of the center's facility will be free for all Springfield residents. The recreation center will have a swimming pool, jogging track, gymnasium and fitness equipment. The banquet facility and conference center will be convenient for area businesses who are looking for a meeting site. It is likely that the Business Association will move its meetings to the facility. Construction is scheduled to begin late this summer.

New factory coming to Springfield

Acme Widget Corporation announced earlier this month that it will be building a new factory in eastern Springfield, providing around 300 new jobs and a boost to the area's economy.

Nominations sought for offices

The annual elections of the Springfield Business Association are scheduled for August 30. If you are interested in running for office or would like to nominate someone, send notice in writing to the association office before July 10. Open offices are president, vice-president, secretary and treasurer. All members in good standing are eligible to run and vote.

Springfield Superstars

Davis receives national award

Henry Davis, president of Davis Printing Services, was recently named Entrepreneur of the Year by the Regional Small Business Leadership Association. Davis, a past president of the Springfield Business Association, balances his time between his business and a variety of volunteer organizations. The printing company is a true family business; Henry's wife and three grown children work there and all play an integral role in making sure things run smoothly.

Davis appreciates the award but is modest about his accomplishments. "A lot of people deserve this more than I do," he says. "I just got lucky. I've got a great family to help me, and I'm filling a need in the Springfield business community."

If you stop in to have some printing done or run into Henry in any of his other pursuits, make sure to offer him your congratulations for this recognition of his achievements.

Chapter Leaders

President:
Martha Birnum
Birnum Communications
555-8258

Vice-President:
Thomas Craddock
Home Hardware
555-2710

Secretary:
Victoria Evans
Springfield Savings Bank
555-4477

Treasurer:
Steven Pauling
Pauling Accounting Services
555-0189

Sidesplitters

When Harvey died, he was given a choice between Heaven and Hell. He arranged to tour both before deciding. Heaven was soft, golden and peaceful. Hell was filled with wild parties, loud music and beautiful women. Harvey chose to go to Hell.

When he arrived, he was thrown to a fiery pit and forced to work all day shoveling brimstone. He asked why everything was so different than it was on the tour. "That's easy," the Devil replied; "then you were a prospect, now you're a customer."

Business School

Make the Internet work for you

The Internet can be an invaluable research tool, but it can also be a huge waste of time. Use these tips to avoid getting stuck in Cyberspace.
- Get on the Net early in the day to avoid high-traffic times
- Upgrade your modem to at least 28.8 bps
- Don't get sidetracked by interesting but irrelevant sites
- Read the "help" files for the search engine you use most often
- Bookmark useful sites for future reference
- If there's reading material you've been meaning to read, glance through it while waiting for large sites to load
- Turn off the graphics capabilities on your browser for really efficient searches

With a little patience and a little common sense, you can make the Internet into an efficient and powerful asset to your business.

For more information on getting online, contact CyberFriends at 555-1234.

How and why to offer fax-on-demand

Whether you have a service- or a product-oriented business, a fax-on-demand system can be an easy, efficient way to get information into customers' hands. You can offer catalogs, price lists, brochures or other information on the systems and then publicize the phone number to customers.

There are two different types: For a call-back system, customers phone in an enter the document number and their fax number. The fax-on-demand system calls them back and transmits the document. For a one-call system, callers phone in from their fax machines, enter the document number and hang up. The system then transmits the document to them immediately. One-call systems are cheaper for the sender but will not work for people who use computer faxes.

Regardless of which system you choose, make sure all information is correct and updated frequently. Test the system periodically for speed and accuracy.

For more information on fax-on-demand services, call The Fax Pros at 555-2020.

"In golf, as in life, it's the follow-through that makes the difference."

unknown

Highlights

Annual golf tournament exceeds goals

The Springfield Business Association's golf tournament was a huge success this year. Good publicity and great weather are credited with the turnout for the event, held at Sunfish Lake Resort on May 3. A record number of entries allowed the Association to raise over $3,000 for charity. Thanks to everyone who came and "took a swing at it." Congratulations to the winning foursome: Dave Collins, Marv Johnson, Al Morgan and Tom Drinnen.

News Stories for Non-Profit Newsletters

In non-profit newsletters, your "News" section reports on condition and trends that show a need for your ongoing services.

Keep section heading as is or select the text and change it to one of the options listed on page 126.

Type in a headline or wait until Step 4.

Create your news article by answering these questions directly on the screen(select over the question and type your answer). Use the questions below to get ideas.

What's New?

Subject of news + action created

(See Step 3 for story ideas) What is the most important thing that has happened since the last newsletter or will happen soon? What do readers need to know about it? What does it involve? What changes will it cause? What is being said about it? Why is it important to readers? Why did it happen?

Who is affected by the story? Who caused it to happen? How will it affect you or your readers? How will it benefit them? How did it happen? Where did it or will it happen? When did it or will it happen?

Tell readers who to call for more information or what action to take.

This is how the "News" section appears on the template.

- ❑ What are legal issues affecting the organization?
- ❑ What legal or legislative issues should members write to representatives about?
- ❑ What can members do in their daily lives to support the organization or its causes?
- ❑ What has been the biggest change in the organization's area of interest in the past year? decade?
- ❑ What changes do you see occurring in the next year? Next decade?
- ❑ What would go on the organization's "wish list?"
- ❑ What are some successes the organization has had recently?
- ❑ What needs to be accomplished and how quickly?
- ❑ How are the issues your organization supports or fights portrayed in popular culture and in the media?

*Plan the content of each new issue using the form **6content.pdf** on the CD. (See a thumbnail of the form on page 31.)*

Ideas for Your News Section

After creating the list, number ideas by priority.

_____

_____

_____

_____

_____

_____

_____

_____

From the Grapevine

Food Bank receives grant

The Springfield Food Bank was awarded a state grant of $15,000, to be paid out over two years. The money will be used to provide much-needed repairs for the delivery vans. This will free up incoming funds for the most pressing need: providing food for underprivileged Springfield citizens. The Food Bank Board is now accepting bids for the van repairs.

Call 555-FOOD (555-3663) to put in a bid.

A completed "News" section from a non-profit newsletter.

51

Keep section heading as is or select the text and change it to one of the options listed on page 126.

Type in a headline or wait until Step 4.

Create your news article by answering these questions directly on the screen(select over the question and type your answer). Use the questions below to get ideas.

People Stories for Non-Profit Newsletters

The "People" section includes profiles, success stories, recognition of volunteers and donors and other messages or letters.

Who's News?

Person in the news + action created

(See Step 3 for story ideas) Whom is it about? Why is this person being spotlighted? Why is it important to readers? How has he or she made a difference? How do readers know this person? How did the subject of the story become involved? What is important about this person? What else has he or she done? What is the person's background? What are his or her plans for the future?

When did this person become involved with the story or the organization? Where did the events being written about occur? Where is the person from? Where did he or she attend school or college?

This is how the "People" section appears on the template.

❑ Who are some people who should be thanked or recognized for contributions, donations, volunteering or work for the organization?

❑ Tell before-and-after stories of the people you've helped.

❑ Explain your most immediate needs.

❑ What are some upcoming volunteer opportunities?

❑ Profile a staff member.

❑ What are some local businesses who support the organization or its causes?

❑ What keeps members, volunteers and staff motivated?

❑ List your board members.

❑ Do you know of any members who've undergone a "conversion" — people who used to be against your cause but changed their minds?

❑ How can you involve children and teenagers in your organization or its causes?

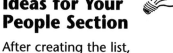

Ideas for Your People Section

After creating the list, number ideas by priority.

_____

_____

_____

_____

_____

_____

_____

_____

A completed "People" section from a non-profit newsletter.

In the Limelight

Davis receives national award

Henry Davis, president of Davis Printing Services, was recently named Entrepreneur of the Year by the Regional Small Business Leadership Association. Davis, a long-time board member and active Food Bank volunteer, was recognize for his ability to balance his time between business and volunteerism. His wife and grown children work in the printing business and also work with the Food Bank in their spare time.

Davis appreciates the award but is modest about his accomplishments. "I'm honored, but a lot of people deserve this more than I do," he says. "I've got great family support, and I'm just glad for the opportunity to support the community. I love my work, and I love helping other people."

Education Stories for Non-Profit Newsletters

The "Education" section includes helpful articles on subjects related to your cause. See page 34 for information on including editorials and letters.

Keep section heading as is or select the text and change it to one of the options listed on page 127.

Type in a headline or wait until Step 4.

Create your news article by answering these questions directly on the screen(select over the question and type your answer). Use the questions below to get ideas.

What Do You Know?

How to + (intended action) + (subject)

(See Step 3 for story ideas) What should readers know? What should they do? What is your connection to this issue or information? What are some facts and opinions that affect readers about this issue? How does the issue affect them? How will it change them? How will it benefit them? Why is it important? Why should readers act on this issue or piece of information? When can it be used? Whom does it affect?

Tell readers who to call for more information or what action to take.

This is how the "Education" section appears on the template.

- ❑ What statistics would be useful for donors and volunteers?
- ❑ List your mission statement in every newsletter.
- ❑ What terms or other jargon should readers be familiar with?
- ❑ What are the top myths or misconceptions about your organization or area of interest?
- ❑ What other publications within your organization should readers know about (Web sites, magazines, brochures, etc.)?
- ❑ What products should members support or boycott?
- ❑ How are dues and donations spent?
- ❑ What are other organizations members should know about?
- ❑ See filler stories for Education sections on page 135.

Ideas for Your Education Section

After creating the list, number ideas by priority.

_____

_____

_____

_____

_____

_____

_____

Food for Thought

Making a difference every day

It's easy to see our accomplishments when we deliver food to the needy, but we can also help out in less obvious ways.

- Stop by and visit with an elderly or shut-in person on your way home from work. Many of these people not only hunger for food but for companionship.
- Donate both money and time to the Food Bank. Both funds and volunteers are necessary to keep us open and running.
- Consider hiring a homeless or needy person if you have an opening in your business or for household help.
- Encourage local restaurants to donate extra food to the Food Bank.
- Patronize business that support the Food Bank.

Turn the time you have available for volunteering into an attitude of service and commitment to helping the community.

A completed "Education" section from a non-profit newsletter.

Keep section heading as is or select the text and change it to one of the options listed on page 127.

What's Happening?

Name of the event
When will it happen?
Where will it happen?
Why is it important to readers?
How to sign up.

Name of the event
When will it happen?
Where will it happen?
Why is it important to readers?
How to sign up.

This is how the "Events" section appears on the template.

Event Listings or Stories for Non-Profit News

List your own events or other upcoming events in your community.

❑ What are some upcoming events?

❑ Report on past events.

❑ What events, such as banquets, meetings, demonstrations, protests and press conferences, are coming up?

❑ What happened at past events such as these?

Entertainment Stories for Non-Profit Newsletters

People need a break from the day's pressures. Include an inspirational or amusing quote, cartoon or story.

❑ Tell a tasteful joke or story you've recently heard.

❑ Include a quote from the CD (see page 131).

❑ Include a trivia question from the CD (see page 132).

❑ Include a cartoon from the CD (see page 129).

Ideas for Your Events Section

After creating the list, number ideas by priority.

_____
_____
_____
_____
_____
_____
_____

Ideas for Your Entertainment Section

After creating the list, number ideas by priority.

_____
_____
_____
_____
_____
_____

News and Notes for Volunteers & Donors from the Springfield Food Bank   Fall XXXX

The Food Chain

Dateline

Benefit Auction
noon, September 10
Springfield Fairgrounds
Donations of goods and services are being accepted and volunteers are being sought.
Call 555-4444 to volunteer or make a donation.

Benefit Dance
7:00 pm, September 25
Homestyle Banquet Center
Tickets: $5 advance, $10 at door. Come and twist, twirl and tango the night away. All proceeds benefit the Food Bank.

Lecture
7:00 pm - 10:00 pm, October 10
YMCA Meeting Room #2
Mark Rollins, internationally recognized expert on organic growth methods, will discuss new techniques in food production. Free.

Office Rehab
10:00 am - 2:00 pm, October 15-17
Food Bank offices
We're looking for volunteers to provide paint, brushes and elbow grease for office renovation.
Call 555-4444 to volunteer.

Springfield Auto Show
5:00 pm - midnight, October 1-5
Springfield Fair Grounds
The Food Bank will have a booth at this annual event. We're looking for people to work the booth -- you'll probably get a call from Andy Cunningham.

From the Grapevine

Food Bank receives grant

The Springfield Food Bank was awarded a state grant of $15,000, to be paid out over two years. The money will be used to provide much-needed repairs for the delivery vans. This will free up incoming funds for the most pressing need: providing food for underprivileged Springfield citizens. The Food Bank Board is now accepting bids for the van repairs.
Call 555-FOOD (555-3663) to put in a bid.

New factory coming to Springfield

ACME Widget Corporation announced earlier this month that it will be building a new factory in eastern Springfield, providing around 300 new jobs and a boost to the area's economy. This will help offset some of the job losses caused by the closing of the XYZ Factory two years ago.

Springfield Book Source turns reading into feeding

John and Helen Murphy, owners of the Springfield Book Source, have made a special offer for the month of October: they will donate 10% of their profits to the Food Bank. Make sure to stop in and fill a shopping bag during that month and thank John and Helen for their generosity.
Springfield Book Source is open from 9 am to 9 pm and is located on the corner of Main and 9th Streets.

In the Limelight

Davis receives national award

Henry Davis, president of Davis Printing Services, was recently named Entrepreneur of the Year by the Regional Small Business Leadership Association. Davis, a long-time board member and active Food Bank volunteer, was recognize for his ability to balance his time between business and volunteerism. His wife and grown children work in the printing business and also work with the Food Bank in their spare time.

Davis appreciates the award but is modest about his accomplishments. "I'm honored, but a lot of people deserve this more than I do," he says. "I've got great family support, and I'm just glad for the opportunity to support the community. I love my work, and I love helping other people."

If you stop in to have some printing done or work with Henry in any Food Bank activities, make sure to offer him your congratulations for this recognition of his achievements and thank him for all the hard work he does for the organization.

Big Cheeses

Springfield Food Bank Board
Chair:
  Carol Watkins
  Health Care Services, Inc.
Vice-chair:
  Andrew Cunningham
  Insurance Advisors
Secretary:
  Marcia Kopetski
  Springfield Savings Bank
Treasurer:
  Virginia Clark
  Pauling Accounting Svcs.
Legal Counsel:
  Alan Singer
  Smith, Singer, Walters
Members:
  Henry, Davis, George
  Martin, Louis North, Betty
  Brown, Amy McGuire,
  Tracy Phillips, Joseph
  Peters, Robert Brown

Mission:
The Springfield Food Bank is a not-for-profit organization dedicated to delivering nutritious meals to Springfield's underprivileged, ill, elderly and shut-in population.

Pulling the Wishbone

Items on the Food Bank Wish List for this quarter:
computer monitor
file cabinets
paint
paintbrushes
copy paper
coffee machine

Food for Thought

Making a difference every day

It's easy to see our accomplishments when we deliver food to the needy, but we can also help out in less obvious ways.
- Stop by and visit with an elderly or shut-in person on your way home from work. Many of these people not only hunger for food but for companionship.
- Donate both money and time to the Food Bank. Both funds and volunteers are necessary to keep us open and running.
- Consider hiring a homeless or needy person if you have an opening in your business or for household help.
- Encourage local restaurants to donate extra food to the Food Bank.
- Patronize business that support the Food Bank.

Turn the time you have available for volunteering into an attitude of service and commitment to helping the community.

That's a Mouthful

"Is it only the mouth and belly which are injured by hunger and thirst? Men's minds are also injured by them."

Meng-tzu, Chinese Philosopher

Apples of Our Eyes

Our loss is Peace Corps' gain

David Franklin, a Food Bank volunteer for four years, is graduating from Springfield State College and joining the Peace Corps. He expects to be sent to Africa, where he will use his degree in agriculture to help farmers increase output by using organic farming methods. While we will miss him, we wish him the best in his future pursuits. Thanks for all your hard work, David.

Former recipient becomes grateful volunteer

If you've spent much time around the Food Bank offices, you've met Mary Dixon. She's the one doing the jobs of three people at once. Mary has volunteered for the Food Bank for two years. Before that, she was a recipient of Food Bank services.

"I had fallen on really hard times right after my husband died," she says. "I don't think my kids and I could have made it without the Food Bank. The food they provided got us through the toughest winter I can imagine."

After Mary was able to find a job and arrange child care for Thomas, Christy and Steven, she knew she wanted to give something back to the people who had helped her when she needed it. Through her tireless volunteer efforts, she has given back more than we could ever have given.

Please note that we usually don't name clients. Mary requested to tell her story in this newsletter.

Ideas for Offers (see page 29)

After creating the list, number ideas by priority.

_____

_____

_____

_____

_____

_____

_____

A sample complete newsletter from a non-profit organization.

*Plan the content of each new issue using the form **6content.pdf** on the CD.*

News Stories for Community Newsletters

In community newsletters, your "News" section reports on issues, trends and news of your school, club, neighborhood, church or family.

For School, Club & Scout Newsletters:

❑ What new classes, programs, clubs or teams have been added recently?

❑ What equipment has been added recently (computers, playground equipment, sports equipment, audio-visual)?

❑ What community issues or legislative issues affect the school?

❑ What trends are affecting the student body?

❑ What are parents' greatest concerns about the schools (crime, drugs, poor grades, etc.) and what is your school doing to address them?

❑ Are there any openings on committees that need to be filled?

❑ When are elections?

❑ What is the club doing to bring in new members and increase community exposure?

❑ How can parents get involved?

❑ What issues are effecting scouting on a national level?

❑ What materials or other items does the troop need?

❑ What is the school, troop or club troop doing to help the community?

❑ What is on your wish list?

For Church Newsletters:

❑ What is your church doing to help the community?

❑ What local or national events might affect your church?

❑ Have there been any important changes to the national or international denomination that would affect your local congregation?

❑ What is your church's mission?

❑ What have been some activities or decisions of committees?

❑ What does the church need help with (donations of money or goods, help with repairs or painting, volunteers for dinners or banquets)?

❑ What committees have openings?

For Neighborhood Newsletters:

❑ What city, state or national issues might affect the community?

❑ Is there any new commercial construction or any store openings that might affect the community?

❑ Are there any proposed construction or zoning issues residents should know about?

❑ What is going on in neighborhood parks or civic centers?

❑ What needs to be done or changed in the neighborhood?

❑ What can neighbors do to help each other?

❑ What is being done to ensure safety in the neighborhood?

❑ What houses are selling at at what price?

❑ Any proposed tax measures that will affect the neighborhood?

For Family Newsletters (see above also)

❑ What family members have had significant events (births, weddings, graduations, anniversaries, deaths, new houses, relocations)?

Ideas for Your News Section

After creating the list, number ideas by priority.

_____

_____

_____

_____

_____

_____

_____

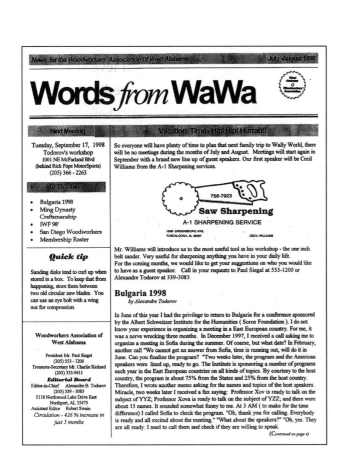

The Woodworkers Association of Western Alabama, WaWa, has used this newsletter to grow its club membership 100 fold.

People Stories for Community Newsletters

The "People" section includes profiles, success stories, recognition of volunteers, welcome messages and other messages or letters.

For School, Club & Scout Newsletters:

❑ Who has been hired recently (teachers, staff, administrators)?

❑ What students deserve recognition for activities or awards in or out of school?

❑ What teams or clubs have achieved successes or received honors?

❑ What opportunities exist for parents to get involved?

❑ Encourage submissions by students — letters or poems, cartoons or question and answer columns.

❑ Who are some "unsung heroes" in your school (secretaries, nurses, maintenance)?

❑ Pick one class or one grade to feature for every issue.

❑ Who are current officers?

What is the responsibility of each officer position?

❑ Has the club or have any members been featured in the news or other media?

❑ List significant events in members' lives — births, weddings, etc.

❑ Profile a club member and include information about job, family, reasons for joining, hometown, other hobbies, etc.

❑ Profile outstanding scouts.

Have any scouts achieved success in school, sports, or other activities?

❑ Who has received honors?

For Church Newsletters:

❑ What members have had significant events or life changes (births, weddings, graduations, anniversaries, deaths)?

❑ Who has joined the church recently?

❑ Have any new staff members been hired?

❑ Who is a "behind-the-scenes hero" in your church or congregation?

❑ Who should be thanked or recognized for hard work or accomplishments?

❑ What members have had accomplishments in other areas of their lives (school, work, sports, etc.)?

❑ "In memory of" mentions

❑ People in hospital or in need of home visits

For Neighborhood Newsletters:

❑ Have any residents experienced significant events (births, weddings, deaths, anniversaries, graduations)?

❑ List new residents.

❑ Give new addresses for people who've moved recently (with permission only).

❑ Endorse local businesses who are loyal or helpful to the community.

❑ Profile local politicians or representatives.

❑ What do residents feel is the biggest challenge or problem affecting the neighborhood?

For Family Newsletters:

❑ Who should be thanked for hard work or accomplishments?

❑ Has the family unofficially "adopted" anyone who is now included in family events? Who is the person? How did he or she come to be included?

❑ Interview the person about his or her impressions of the family.

❑ Profile a family member, maybe a patriarch or matriarch, maybe a less well-known member of the family or someone who has moved away.

❑ List addresses and phone numbers of family members who've moved recently.

❑ Ask people their memories of a family member who has passed away.

❑ Ask spouses of family members for their first impressions of the family and how those may have changed over the years.

Ideas for Your People Section

After creating the list, number ideas by priority.

_____

_____

_____

_____

_____

_____

Ideas for Your Education Section

After creating the list, number ideas by priority.

_____

_____

_____

_____

_____

_____

Education Stories for Community Newsletters

The "Education" section includes helpful articles on subjects of interest to your readers. See page 34 for information on including editorials and letters.

❑ See filler stories for Education sections on page 135 .

For School, Club & Scout Newsletters:

❑ What can parents do to ensure learning continues at home?

❑ What books or computer software can you recommend to parents for their children to read and learn from?

❑ What other publications would members be interested in?

❑ What are the benefits of membership?

❑ Report on the history of the club. Who founded it? How many original members were there? Are any original members still involved?

❑ How long has the troop been in existence?

For Church Newsletters:

❑ What is the history of your church? When was it founded? When was the building built?

❑ What books or movies should members be aware of?

❑ How are decisions made within the congregation?

❑ What statistics should members know (number of members, growth in membership, budget)?

❑ What educational opportunities exist within the church for teachers or students (Sunday Schools, Bible Schools, conferences, seminars, etc.)?

For Neighborhood Newsletters:

❑ What is the history of the neighborhood?

❑ Who in the neighborhood has lived there the longest?

For Family Newsletters:

❑ What is the history of the family? How long in this country? Where did the family originate? What does the name mean?

❑ What wisdom, knowledge or skills have been passed down the generations?

Event Listings or Stories for Community Newsletters

The "Events" section lists your own events or other upcoming events in your community.

For School, Club & Scout Newsletters:

❑ List upcoming banquets, picnics or other events.

❑ Report on past events.

❑ What events are coming up?

❑ Report on past events?

❑ Encourage people to stay current with dues.

For Church Newsletters:

❑ What events are coming up?

❑ Report on past events.

❑ What is happening with children or youth groups?

❑ What holidays or seasons are coming up?

For Neighborhoods:

❑ Are there any meetings coming up?

❑ What activities or events are there for children in the neighborhood?

❑ Are there any organized activities such as bingo, softball, soccer, or other games or sports for people of all ages in the neighborhood?

❑ Report on past meetings.

For Family Newsletters:

❑ What family events are coming up (holidays, picnics, reunions, parties)?

❑ What happened at the last family event?

❑ Ask people their earliest memories of holidays or family reunions.

❑ What is the funniest thing that has happened at a family event?

❑ What family stories get told at every event?

❑ Who tells the most stories? Who tells the most jokes?

❑ What foods are included at every event? Who makes them?

Keep section heading as is or select the text and change it to one of the options listed on page 127.

What's Happening?

Name of the event
When will it happen?
Where will it happen?
Why is it important to readers?
How to sign up.

Name of the event
When will it happen?
Where will it happen?
Why is it important to readers?
How to sign up.

This is how the "Events" section appears on the template.

Ideas for Your Events Section

After creating the list, number ideas by priority.

_____

_____

_____

_____

_____

_____

_____

Entertainment Stories for Community Newsletters

People need a break from the day's pressures. Include an inspirational or amusing quote, cartoon or story anywhere within the newsletter.

Ideas for Your Entertainment Section

After creating the list, number ideas by priority.

_____

_____

_____

_____

_____

_____

_____

_____

❑ Include a quote from the CD (see page 131).

❑ Include a trivia question from the CD (see page 132).

❑ Include a cartoon from the CD (see page 129).

For School, Club & Scout Newsletters:

❑ What are the most popular songs, movies, books among students of different ages? Among teachers, administrators, staff?

For Neighborhoods:

❑ Print a recipe.

❑ What famous person would you like to see move in?

❑ Are any famous people from or have any famous people visited your neighborhood?

❑ Have a contest in which people name an official song, tree and bird for the neighborhood.

❑ What pets are most known in the neighborhood?

❑ What wild animals are seen the most?

❑ Print classified ads for people who have things to sell.

❑ Are there any neighborhood garages sales coming up?

For Family Newsletters:

❑ Print a recipe of an important family food, if the chef is willing to tell.

❑ What keepsakes or mementos have been in the family for many years?

❑ Have there been any famous members of the family?

❑ Do you know of any interesting, perhaps eccentric, ancestors?

❑ Does anyone have an unusual hobby, job or pet?

❑ Who within the family has the most children?

❑ Who are the oldest and youngest members of the family?

❑ What celebrity should be but isn't a member of the family?

❑ List classifieds—family collection items/swaps.

News to Know for Parents & Students of the Springfield School District — Spring XXXX

Springfield Scoop

Exciting Events

Spring Dance
7:00 pm to midnight, April 15
Springfield H.S. Gymnasium
Juniors and Seniors are invited to
attend the annual dance. This
year's theme: Nostalgia

PTO Meeting
6:30 pm - 8:00 pm, May 1
H.S. Library Meeting Room

Spring Band Concert
7:00 pm - 9:00 pm, May 12
H.S. Auditorium
A special ceremony honoring Dr.
Hopkins will take place during the
concert.

5th Grade Play
7:00 pm - 8:00 pm, May 20
Grade School Gym
Watch the 5th-graders perform
"The Wizard of Oz."

Graduation Ceremonies
Kindergarten: noon, June 3
5th Grade: 3:00 pm, June 3
Elementary School Gym

8th Grade: 3:00 pm, June 6
Junior High Gym

High School:
Baccalaureate:
*   6:00 pm, June 17*
Graduation:
*   8:00 pm, June 17*
Football Field

Telling Tales Out of School

High school to add new wing

In February, Springfield voters passed a large bond issue that will allow the high school to add a new science wing with labs and a computer center. Once the computer center is completed, the school will go online, with Internet connections and a home page. The school is taking bids for the new construction, which is expected to be finished at the end of next year. Principal Harris says, "We're really excited about the changes we can implement with these funds. I'd like to thank the Springfield voters for their recognition of the necessity of voting yes for our schools."

Baseball star to speak at high school graduation

The graduating class will have the honor of meeting Terry Collins, starting left fielder for the Kansas City Royals, when he delivers the address for the graduation ceremonies on June 17. Collins is a 1992 graduate of Springfield High and went on to play baseball at State University before being picked up by the Royals. A limited number of tickets for graduation are set aside for Springfield residents who are not family members of graduating students.

Call 555-2700 for ticket information.

Talent Show

Band director announces retirement

Dr. Frank Hopkins, who has led the high school band for 30 years, announced early in the spring that he will be retiring this year. Under his guidance, the band has placed in the top three slots in the State Contest 10 times, and band members have won more than 30 individual awards. His retirement is a big loss for the school, but students, administrators and parents wish him the best in his retirement.

Eighth-grader wins State Spelling Bee

Mary Buchanan, an eighth-grader in Mrs. Miller's class at Springfield Middle School, won the State Spelling Bee on March 22. Congratulations to Mary for her hard work and accomplishment in knowing how to correctly spell "pseudonymity" (the fact or state of being signed with a pseudonym).

New track coach hired

Nicole Thorn has been hired as the new coach for the high school women's cross-country team. Nicole is a graduate of State University, where she competed in track and cross-country. She says her goal is to lead the Springfield High School women's team to the State Championships within 3 years.

Kids' Corner

From Katie Walker (Mr. Delgado's 3rd grade class)
Q: What did the snail say when he was riding on the turtle's back?
A: WHEEEE!

From Michael Blaine (Ms. Schmidt's 1st grade class)
Q: What did the glass of water say to the ice cube?
A: You're pretty cool.

From Sarah Morris (Miss Allen's 4th grade class)
Q: If a red house is made of red wood and a blue house is made of blue wood, what is a green house made of?
A: Glass!

Sports Highlights

*Baseball: Sophomore **James Greene** was named to the County All-Star team.*

*Track & Field: The **boys' mile relay team** set a new school record at the District Meet on March 30.*

*Basketball: **Tony Cooper** set a record for most points (32) in one game on Feb. 10 against Clayton.*

*Wrestling: Senior **David Griffin** won a scholarship to the University of Wisconsin.*

Back to School

How to instill a love of reading in your child

In this age of cable TV, computers and video games, parents often wonder what they can do to teach their children to enjoy books. The most important thing you can do is to share their reading with them. Try these tips:

- Read *to* younger children and *with* older ones every day
- Make sure your children see you reading
- Vary your reading to include magazines, books and newspapers
- Discuss books with your children; ask them what happened in their stories
- Take children to the library or to bookstores
- Encourage children to join book clubs or reading groups
- Treat reading as a reward, not as homework

If kids learn to love reading early, the habit will stay with them throughout their lives.

PTO offers Internet pamphlet

For parents who are interested in or concerned about the Internet, the PTO is offering a pamphlet that spells out the basics of the Information Superhighway. Parents can see how their children can use the Internet wisely for education and research and learn how to keep their children safe from the hazards of cyberspace.

Call Mary Brown at 555-2883 for information.

Classroom Connection

Mrs. VanAllen's class discovers the Bard

The students in Mrs. VanAllen's Sophomore English class don't just read about a subject, they live it. For their Shakespeare unit last semester, the students studied life in Elizabethan England, wrote speeches in Shakespearean English, attended a production of *Hamlet* at the Springfield Community Theater and performed a scene from *As You Like It* for the student body. For their performance, they wore authentic costumes and recruited band members to perform Elizabethan music. For the final project, each student chose a character from a Shakespearean play and answered questions from the rest of the class about what he or she did in the play and why.

Ideas for Offers (see page 29)

After creating the list, number ideas by priority.

_____

_____

_____

_____

_____

_____

_____

_____

A sample community newsletter from a school.

Safety Tips and Trends for Laboratory Employees from Gile and Associates

Safety Savvy

Volume 1, Number 1   July, 1998

The Nitty-Gritty

Section (g)(2)(vii)(N0 of the Bloodborne Pathogen states that here must be "an opportunity for interactive questions and answers with a person conducting the training session". OSHA has interpreted that language to mean that if a generic program is used (even an interactive computer program), it must be accessible for interaction.

Whether or not the use of telephone access for the Q&A period would depend on accessibility and the ratio of trainers answering the phone to number of employees calling.

If the training is performance and/or competency based, compliance officers will determine on a case-by-case basis whether the training is effective and adequate.

This is accomplished through observation of work practices and employee interview to determine that the training is presented in a manner that is appropriate to the employees' education, literacy level, and language. ▼

◆◆◆◆◆◆◆◆◆◆◆◆◆◆◆◆◆◆◆

Safety Savvy is published 10 times per year. For a subscription, send a check or money order for $15 to Gile and Associates, 11339 Oak Branch Drive, St. Louis, MO 63128-1408.

Editorial Expressions

Welcome !

Terry Jo Gile, Editor

This is the first issue of *Safety Savvy*, a newsletter for Laboratory employees devoted to safety issues. This newsletter will keep you up-to-date on safety regulations as well as inform you of the latest safety information and innovations (see **What's Hot and What's Not !**). In addition, we will have frequently asked questions (see **Just The FAQs**) as well as information that you request or submit (see **In The Spotlight**) and an editorial (see **Editorial Expressions**).

This is your newsletter. We want to hear from you! Send your questions, comments, or concerns to: SAFETY SAVVY by fax to (314) 362-2097 or e-mail at tjgile@worldnet.att.net. ▼

What's Hot and What's Not

Latex Allergies

*Karen L. Thurlow, RNC, BSN **

Although we associate latex allergies in the workplace from the latex gloves we wear, in fact, latex can be in a variety of products we use everyday. Items include, but are not limited to, balloons, pencil erasers, rubber baby bottle nipples, rubber pacifiers, rubber bands, Kooch balls, tires, backing on carpet, sports equipment, tub mats, chewing gum, and the scratch off on instant lottery tickets. In the health care setting latex is found in latex gloves, [...] Band-Aids. Even certain foods [...] protein that is similar in composit[...] have an allergic reaction to these [...] of the general population and u[...] sensitivity. ▼

* Karen Thurlow is a Registered Liaison for Northern Diagnostic [...] been active with Latex Allergies [...] age of three. She is intereste[...] professional basis and a persona[...]

Did You Know

OSHA violations for compressed gases fall into the following categories:

1. Stored oxygen cylinders must be separated from fuel-gas cylinders.
2. Cylinders must be secured when stored either by chains or other stabilizing platforms.
3. Valve protection caps must be in place.
4. Oxygen cylinders cannot be stored near combustible materials.

◆◆◆◆◆◆◆◆◆◆◆◆◆◆◆◆◆◆

Ergonomics

The American National Standards Institute (ANSI) has published a voluntary ergonomics standard in lieu of a forthcoming Standard from OSHA. To obtain a copy call (800) 621-7619.

◆◆◆◆◆◆◆◆◆◆◆◆◆◆◆◆◆◆

In the Spotlight

Check out the following web pages for safety related information:

OSHA – *www.osha.gov*

Latex Allergies
http://members.aol.com/Latexfree/index.html

ANSI Ergonomics –
www.nsc.org/z365.htm

Just The FAQs *

* Frequently Asked Questions

1. What is a N-95 mask and why do I have to be face fitted for it?

The N-95 mask was developed in response to the Centers for Disease Control (CDC) published guidelines for protection of employees who come in contact with Tuberculosis (TB). The research arm of CDC called the National Institute for Occupational Safety and Health (NIOSH) established the parameters for the N-95 mask and other respirators. These masks are to be worn when working with a TB patient (eg: phlebotomy, etc.) or when plating or reading cultures of TB (eg: in Microbiology). Each employee who is required to wear this type of mask must be face fitted before being assigned to an area that requires its use. Face fitting for N-95 masks is a requirement and needs to be done only once unless there is structural changes to the face. Other types of respirator masks must be face fitted annually. ▼

"Remember to think and act safely everyday at work, home or play!"

2. Why does a phlebotomist have to change gloves and wash their hands between patients even when the gloves have no blood splashes?

According to a letter date 4/6/93 from Charles Adkins, Director of Health Standards Programs for the Occupational Safety and Health Administration (OSHA), The Bloodborne Pathogen Standard requires that employees wash their hands with soap and water between glove changes and between patient contacts. Handwashing has long been recognized as a basic infection control concept. The Center for Disease Control (CDC) has published a guideline that states that handwashing is indicated even when gloves are used since the gloves may become perforated during use and because bacteria can multiply rapidly on gloved hands. OSHA follows the CDC published guidelines.▼

3. Are there any needleproof gloves available for phlebotomy?

The American Society for Testing and Materials (ASTM) has recently adopted a standardized cut protection performance test (CPPT) which measures the cut resistance of a material by measuring its ability to resist the cutting action of a sharp blade. The lab data shows that cut protection increases with fabric weight. Reinforced yarns provide the best protection with para-aramid and extended chain polyethylene fibers a close second. Cotton and leather are 3rd and 4th respectively. These gloves are very thick and bulky and are reusable rather than disposable as required by OSHA. They would not allow for proper palpitation of the vein or any other fine motor work required in laboratories. They were designed to prevent cuts from glass in housekeeping personnel. There are also mesh gloves that can be worn under other gloves that provide cut resistance but because they are mesh they do not provide protection from small, sharp needles. Victoria Fraser, MD, Washington University Department of Internal Medicine and Infectious Diseases states that glove companies continue to invest in research to develop a puncture proof glove that meets the criteria needed in the laboratory but to date none are available. Needle safety devices and phlebotomy skill still are the best protection available. ▼

Safety expert Terry Jo Gile sells subscriptions to her newsletter, *Safety Savvy.*

Electrifying Editing

estimated time: 20 minutes

By answering the questions on the screen in Step 3, your stories naturally unfold into straight news style. They now contain most of the necessary information. Next, if possible, give yourself a little break from the story. Grab a snack. Run a quick errand.

IN THIS CHAPTER:
- ➤ Review and revise stories
- ➤ Write headlines
- ➤ Write opening sentences
- ➤ Lengthen or shorten articles

Quick-Glance Review

Now, return to your stories for a quick review and revision. Read each one from the viewpoint of the reader while considering these questions:

- ❑ Can I immediately tell what makes this story news?
- ❑ Who should read it?
- ❑ Do I see a clear benefit to reading it?
- ❑ Is there any information that I find unnecessary?
- ❑ Is there anything left out that needs to go in?
- ❑ What other details will make the story more interesting? (Consider including quotes, specific details, testimonials.)

Add any interesting facts into the stories. Then, turn your attention to the most important writing you do: the headline.

Show-Stopping Headlines

Readers skim through headlines. You need to communicate as much as possible. Now, note the difference between a title and a headline. "Hamlet" is a title. "Prince Sees Ghost, Kills King" is a headline. Hang onto your press hats. Here's how to create terrific headlines.

Most headlines contain subjects and verbs. This is how dull headlines—"Employee Update"—can be converted to action heads—"Profit-Sharing Checks on the Way." If it's needed for organization of the news, use "Employee Update" as a section head. Capture the benefit of the story. Show why someone should take the time to read the article.

Verbs for News:

presents, offers, introduces, expands, adds, unveils, wins, unfurls, opens, initiates, launches, ushers in, provides, highlights, starts, names, surpasses, achieves, accomplishes, earns, obtains, acquires, reaches, succeeds, declares

Verbs for Educational Articles and Offers:

decreases, lowers, cuts, phases out, reduces, avoids, eliminates, diminishes, lessens, minimizes

lengthens, increases, extends, enhances, upgrades, lifts, expands, grows, develops, multiplies, raises, improves

learns, uses, discovers, uncovers, utilizes

Other Educational Headlines:

How to get your money's worth on high-tech equipment

What every parent should know about education

The ten most common sales mistakes ... and how to avoid them

WORKSHEET: Whipping Headlines Into Shape

The easiest way to write a **News** headline is:

Subject	+ Verb	+ Direct Object
Customer	saves	millions
Conference	highlights	growth in industry
Acme	doubles	plant size

Your turn:

_____ _____ _____

_____ _____ _____

_____ _____ _____

_____ _____ _____

_____ _____ _____

The easiest way to write an **Educational** or **Offer** headline is:

Verb	+ Object
Fix	financial fears forever
Eliminate	tuition worries with new savings plan
Keep	kids active during summer months
Pack	more into each day with time-saving tips

Your turn:

_____ _____

_____ _____

_____ _____

_____ _____

_____ _____

How to + (intended action) + (subject)	Subject of news + action created

Change these headlines that are on your screen to the ones you've created above.

| | Person in the news + action created |

Before: New subdivision opens off Highway 100
After: New subdivision saves hours of commute time

Before: New factory coming to Springfield
After: New factory creates buyers' market

More Headline Tips

Write verbs in present tense. It doesn't matter if the event has already passed.

past: Customer saved millions

present: Customer saves millions

past The countdown to relocation has begun

present: The countdown to relocation begins

Alliteration. Advertising research has shown that alliterative headlines make an ad 30 to 40 percent more memorable. The easiest way to work alliteration into your headlines is to match the first letter of the verb in the headline with the object (direct or indirect). Here are some examples:

Countdown to the convention

Fix financial fears forever

Tell us your travel tips

Rhymes and puns. Rhymes and puns can work in headlines... but remember the sage advice of Greek physician Galen, "The dose makes the poison." Avoid overusing pun and rhyme headlines and never use them for serious news articles.

Pun headlines work best for educational articles such as "Home Neat Home." Rhymes can also work for event announcement headlines such as, "Hip Hip Hooray! More Fun Comin' Your Way!"

Writing Lead Sentences

If you have 15 minutes, try out some imaginative openings (leads) for the story. If not, skip to page 69.

The job of the lead is to:
- ❑ capture readers' attention
- ❑ contain the most unique, most important or most unusual item in story
- ❑ include readers or their interests
- ❑ focus on most newsworthy point of story
- ❑ establish tone and mood of story

Headline Styles

The capitalization of your headline will affect its look.

downstyle:
Prince sees ghost, kills king

uppercase/lowercase:
Prince Sees Ghost, Kills King

all-capital letters (avoid this style):
PRINCE SEES GHOST, KILLS KING

Note:

Don't use a period at the end of headlines.

"Who handles your media, Rex?"

Types of Leads

Straight news—Dives right in to heart of story with facts and details.

"Acme threw a blowout bash for the grand opening of its new store last month."

Benefit lead—Tells readers what's in it for them.

"Cut your air conditioning bills in half. No, not with scissors. With the right landscaping."

Straight talk—Uses "you" or "we" to speak directly to readers and their interests.

"If you've ever imagined waking up one day $1,000,000 dollars richer, you can relate to John Smith's success story."

Problem/solution—Outlines the problem, explain how to fix it.

"Every year, there are more physical therapists competing for fewer jobs, but graduates of the State University Master's program have their pick of positions."

Narrative or description—Tells a story, describes an event, creates a mental image.

"When John Smith was a baby, doctors told his parents he would never walk, but thanks to their determination and the technological advancements at Springfield Hospital, John went on to win medals in track and cross-country."

Question—Involves readers by asking them an intriguing question that the article goes on to answer.

"How does a 39-year-old woman with 3 kids and a full-time job find the time to run 15 miles a day, every day?"

Quotation—Introduces the theme of the article with someone else's words.

A great man once wrote, "Not to oversee the workman is to leave your purse open." The man was Benjamin Franklin, who knew that getting the most for your money requires thorough planning and careful supervision.

Startling fact—Gives a shocking fact or statistic to show the story's importance.

"More collect calls are placed on Father's Day than any other day of the year."

Note:

Try adding a catchy opening sentence to one or two of your articles.

Note:

See *The Newsletter Editor's Handbook* (listed on the back cover) for more information on news writing and editing.

Making Stories More Lively

If the story is too short or you'd like to make it more lively, look for places to add details.

- ❑ Show, rather than tell, readers what you want them to know.
- ❑ Quote someone who has participated in the project or event.
- ❑ Use concrete words.
- ❑ Include details.
- ❑ When applicable and appropriate, use words that engage the senses.
- ❑ Use strong, active verbs.

Making Stories Shorter

Brevity is paramount in newsletter writing. The brevity of newsletters leaves readers feeling that they have gained maximum information in a minimum amount of time. Busy people like this pace.

If a story is too long, you can either shorten it, remove other articles or increase the size from letter-sized to legal-size. When looking for places to shorten the story:

- ❑ include as much of the story as possible in the headline, and don't repeat it in the first paragraph
- ❑ plunge right into the subject in the lead sentence
- ❑ cut extraneous words and shorten sentences.
- ❑ Use pronouns and abbreviations. In a second reference, "personal computer" shortens to "PC," "Wallingford B. Smith" becomes "he," and the "University of California at Irvine" reduces to "UCI," "the university" or "it."
- ❑ Look for single words to replace phrases. Use "now" in place of "at the present time." Replace "in order to" with "to."
- ❑ Don't repeat quoted information. If you have quotes in your articles, you do not need to summarize the information outside the quote.
- ❑ After cutting unnecessary details and sentences, look for places where your writing is too wordy.
- ❑ Look for words to cut. Avoid weak phrases like "there is" or "there are," particularly at the beginnings of sentences. Reword these sentences.

Note:

The steps of adding interest to a story and then editing it for length may seem contradictory, but they should be separate but equally important processes for making sure your stories are read and remembered.

Before:

In this modern age of technology, a great number of people feel confused and overwhelmed by the changes that are occurring at an alarming rate in high-tech communications. For the man or woman who does not want to feel left behind as the work environment keeps constantly changing, there are many places that provide training and instruction for how to utilize new equipment for the best efficiency and highest degree of time management. Acme is one such company.

79 words and not enough concrete information

After:

Acme's training helps people keep up with changes in high-tech communications.

12 words

Before:

There are many reasons why people join our association, such as networking and educational opportunities.

15 words and weak

After:

Our members benefit from networking and educational opportunities.

8 words and strong

Magnetic Mailing Areas

estimated time: 10 minutes

I f you're going to mail your newsletter and aren't going to use envelopes, it's time to set up the mailing panel. If you're going to mail your newsletter in an envelope, hand it out or e-mail it,, skip to Step 6, page 75.

If you're doing a letter-sized newsletter, leave room to tape the mailing panel on the back page. Add paragraph returns until there's room left in the left column. Keep your back page text in the right column short enough to leave room to paste on the panel.

IN THIS CHAPTER:

➤ Select your mailing panel style

➤ Create a teaser to encourage people to open it

➤ Print it, trim it, flip it, paste it

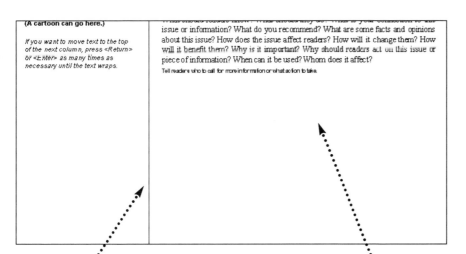

(A cartoon can go here.)

If you want to move text to the top of the next column, press <Return> or <Enter> as many times as necessary until the text wraps.

issue or information? What do you recommend? What are some facts and opinions about this issue? How does the issue affect readers? How will it change them? How will it benefit them? Why is it important? Why should readers act on this issue or piece of information? When can it be used? Whom does it affect?

Tell readers who to call for more information or what action to take.

Fred brings home one cute refrigerator magnet too many.

Note:

Ignore the line separating the columns. The mailing panel will paste over it and conceal it.

Note:

Leave about three inches at the bottom of the last page of your newsletter for the mailing panel.

Two different designs are available on the disk. Open up the design of your choice now.

mailpnl1:

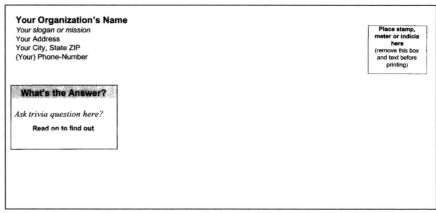

This is the standard mailing panel design.

mailpnl2:

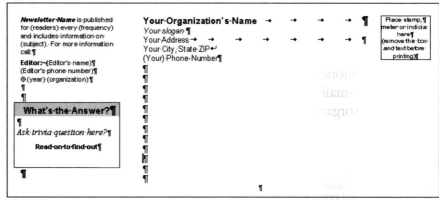

This design includes a masthead (see next page).

What to Put in Your Return Address

Readers will glance to see whom your newsletter is from before they will open it. Include your:

- ❑ organization's name
- ❑ organization's slogan or short mission statement
- ❑ address
- ❑ phone number

Note:

Text will shift around on the screen as you're typing. Use the return and backspace or delete keys to reposition the text.

MS-Word: *mailpnl1.doc or mailpnl2.doc*

WordPerfect: *mailpnl1.wpd or mailpnl2.wpd*

MS-Works: *mailpnl.wps*

Springfield Business Association
Helping businesses grow
123 W. Main St.
Springfield, US 00001
(555) 555-1111

What's Inside?

> *Meeting news*
> *Getting on the Internet*
> *Marketing by fax*

Create a Masthead as a Return Address

If you use the design file mailpnl2, you can set up a simple masthead as part of the return address. Many readers look to the masthead for information on how to contact you or to be put on your mailing list. The following masthead can be used in place of your return address:

(Newsletter Name) is published for (readers) every (frequency) and includes information on (subject). For information call:

Editor: (Editor's name)
(Editor's phone number)
(Editor's e-mail address)
© (year) (organization)

© Tip

To get the "©" symbol in any Windows program, press Alt + 0169.

Business Buzz is published for Springfield businesses every month and includes information to help businesses grow. For more information call:
Editor: Susan Anthony
555-1234
© 2002 Springfield Bus. Assn.

Springfield Business Association
Helping businesses grow
123 W. Main St.
Springfield, US 00001
(555) 555-1111

What's the Answer?

What sport is the subject of the most Hollywood films?
Read on to find out

What Else to Put Here

The first place readers look is at their name on the label. Place something catchy to the left of it. Intrigue and entice readers. Get them to open the newsletter right then. Use any of these:

- ❑ an ad for a sale
- ❑ a short announcement
- ❑ a teaser for the offer you've put on the reply card (see next page, Step 6)
- ❑ the date of your next meeting
- ❑ a message line on the label above the person's name
- ❑ a box listing the contents of the newsletter
- ❑ a cartoon or clip art image
- ❑ a trivia question with a note saying the answer is inside

How to Print and Flip

Once you've set up your mailing area the way you want, print it, trim it to roughly 3 1/2 inches, flip it, and tape, glue or paste it to the bottom of the last page of your newsletter.

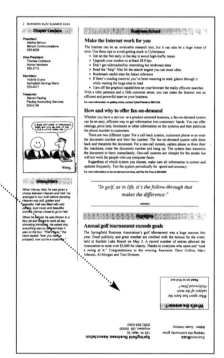

Legal-sized page with mailing area.

How to Fold & Seal

Do not staple your newsletter closed. Staples increase the chances of an equipment jam. Even if the piece survives the postal service, few readers will use a staple remover so they'll end up tearing it. If you want to seal your newsletter— the post office doesn't require it—use a wafer seal or tape.

Letter-sized page with mailing area.

The post office recommends placing two wafer seals—one to the top left and one to the top right. Fold your newsletter so that it is open at the top of the mailing area and folded at the bottom. (See illustration of seals and fold below).

Responsive Reply Cards

O pen up two-way dialogs by turning passive readers into active participants. Your newsletter is a one-way form of communication—unless you get reader response. And most readers won't give you a response unless you ask for it.

Response devices are as simple as a phone number to call or an address to write to. The action lines you crafted in Step 3 work as response-generating devices. Many newsletters go further and include a reply card or RSVP form.

IN THIS CHAPTER:
➤ Craft your offer
➤ Increase your response rate
➤ Fitting it all on

reply:

Yes. I want to learn more about (your subject here). Please send me the (free offering) today.

Hurry. This offer expires (mo/day/year).

(Your Organization)
(Address)
(City St Zip)
(Phone, Fax)

Name _____
Organization _____
Address _____
City, State ZIP _____

Send right away by: ☐ mail ☐ e-mail _____
☐ fax: (   ) _____ ☐ phone (   ) _____

Please also send information on:
☐ item 1   ☐ item 2
☐ item 3   ☐ item 4
☐ item 5   ☐ item 6

This is a reply card for an offer.

rsvp:

Yes. Save my spot at the (date or name) meeting.

Hurry. Your RSVP must be in by (month/day).

Name _____
Organization _____
Address _____
City, State ZIP _____
Phone (   ) _____

Send right away by:
☐ mail : (Your Organization's Name, Address, City, St ZIP)
☐ e-mail : (Your e-mail address)
☐ fax : (Your fax number)
☐ phone : (Your phone number)

This is a reply card for an RSVP.

MS-Word: reply.doc
MS-Word: rsvp.doc
WordPerfect: reply.wpd
WordPerfect: rsvp.wpd
MS-Works: reply.wps
MS-Works: rsvp.wps

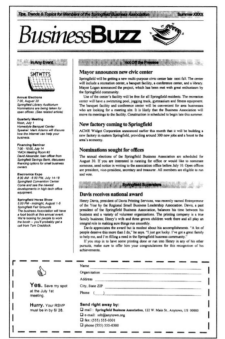

The reply card can be taped to a letter-sized newsletter to create a legal sized page.

Or, you can leave room (3 inches plus 1/2 inch for the bottom margin) at the bottom of a legal-sized newsletter for it to be taped or pasted (the old fashioned way—with scissors and glue) to the page before you make photocopies.

What to Offer

Here are some questions that will help you craft an offer:

- ❏ Do you offer trials, demonstrations or samples?
- ❏ Are you offering any special pricing or discounts?
- ❏ Do you have an upcoming sale?
- ❏ Are you holding a special event soon?
- ❏ Do people need to RSVP for the event?
- ❏ Do you have any closeouts or remainders?
- ❏ Is there anything that lends itself to a money-saving coupon?
- ❏ Do you have any special reports, white papers, copies of handouts or article reprints you can offer to readers?
- ❏ Can you offer a free evaluation of their current products/services?
- ❏ Do you offer free consultations?
- ❏ Do you have any t-shirts, mugs or caps to give away?
- ❏ Do you have anything left over in your supply closet that you can give to readers?
- ❏ What about holding a drawing or contest for a free hour of services or a free product?
- ❏ For neighborhoods or churches, what about offering a recipe or holding a cooking contest?
- ❏ Do you offer free seminars for your prospects?
- ❏ Can you offer information on some or all of your services? (Listing your other services reminds readers of the other capabilities you have.)

Yes. I want to learn more about tax changes for 2005. Please send me your free report today.

Hurry. This offer expires (6/1/04).

Send to:
The Tax Specialists
100 N. Market St.
Anytown, US 00002
(555) 555-0100,
fax: (555) 555-0200

Name _____

Organization _____

Address _____

City, State ZIP _____

Send right away by: ❏ mail ❏ e-mail _____
❏ fax: (   ) _____ ❏ phone (   ) _____

Please also send information on:
❏ estate planning   ❏ retirement accounts
❏ audit representation   ❏ business accounting systems
❏ debt management   ❏ tax shelters

Sample reply card from an accountant.

Icon Tip

To change the "thumbs up" graphic, see the Character Map in Windows for other WingDings characters.

👍

Yes. Save my spot at the July 1st meeting.

Hurry. Your RSVP must be in by 6/28.

Name _____

Organization _____

Address _____

City, State ZIP _____

Phone ( ) _____

Send right away by:

❑ mail : **Springfield Business Association,** 123 W. Main St., Anytown, US 00001
❑ e-mail: ssb@anytown.org
❑ fax: (555) 555-0301
❑ phone (555) 555-1111

Sample RSVP from an association.

How to Increase Response

You can easily double your response to your offer by including the following items on your card.

❑ Offer something of value, something that people want or think is really interesting.

❑ Mention it within an article or action line in the newsletter.

❑ Repeat the offer in a benefit-oriented, active headline (see writing headlines on page 65).

❑ List a deadline for the offer or state "while quantities last."

❑ Repeat your address, phone, fax, e-mail and Web site (the card will get separated from the rest of the newsletter).

❑ Provide check boxes.

❑ Frame the offer in a dashed border.

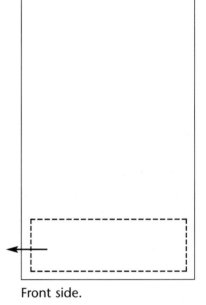

Front side.

If you use the legal-size newsletter with the mailing area on the opposite side of the card, the mailing address for the newsletter stays with the card (see illustration). You can also ask people to staple or tape their business card onto the form to save time.

Have a system in place for processing the requests and getting the materials back to people as quickly as possible. Stamp or print the envelopes containing the promised materials with something like "here's the information you requested."

Back side.

Picture-Perfect Production

estimated time: 20 minutes

I f you're in the mood for a few last-minute tweaks, glance at your newsletter and note the following areas to see if you can create a custom design. (If not, move on to the next page.)

IN THIS CHAPTER:
➤ Getting it perfect
➤ Getting it proofread
➤ Getting it printed
➤ Getting it mailed
➤ Getting ready for next time

Getting It Perfect

Does your company have guidelines for design? Many larger organizations strive to use the same fonts in everything they produce. Ask your public relations or communications department if your organization has such guidelines. If you have the fonts on your computer, try changing change the body text and headline styles in the Style Sheets.

Try changing the body text to a less formal font such as Garamond. Change the body text to "align left" instead of "justified." Note that changing the justification may cause your text to become too long.

If you have certain colors for your organization and have the budget for two color printing, sketch a copy of your newsletter to specify using your color in the following areas. Give this "mock-up" copy to your printer.

Prints blue

If you want your printing service to use a second ink color when printing your document, make a copy of the original and mark on this copy where you'd like the ink color to appear.

Eye halve a spelling chequer
It came with my pea sea
It plainly marques four my revue
Miss steaks eye kin knot sea.
Eye strike a key and type a word
And weight four it two say
Weather eye am wrong oar write
It shows me strait a weigh.
As soon as a mist ache is maid
It nose bee fore two long
And eye can put the error rite
Its rare lea ever wrong.
Eye have run this poem threw it
I am shore your pleased two no
Its letter perfect awl the weigh
My chequer tolled me sew.

-Sauce unknown

*For help with proofreading, see the form **proof.pdf** on the CD.*

Find Service Donations

For nonprofit organizations, donations by printers can greatly offset the costs of publishing. Depending on your mailing list, a mention in the masthead may be excellent advertising for a printer. Ask about using the printer's leftover paper and find a time when the shop is usually not busy to print your newsletter.

Getting It Proofread

Most newsletter editors learn about the importance of proofreading and fact checking the hard way. Cut your learning curve by following these steps. First, if you haven't already done so, use your spelling checker.

Next, hand or fax your newsletter to someone who will proofread it for you. If you don't know anyone who's a good proofreader, look in the Yellow Pages under "Secretarial Services" and find a service who will proof for you via fax.

Proofreading Checklist

Hand or fax this to your proofreader and ask for a focus on these areas.

❑ Read everything once-through for an overall feel.
❑ Read through for punctuation and spelling.
❑ Read all articles and headlines aloud.
❑ Read headlines and most visible text backwards.
❑ Check spelling of all names and company names.
❑ Call phone numbers to verify.
❑ Confirm the date of the newsletter.
❑ Confirm the date of the copyright notice.
❑ Is everything that has been taped on (logos, mailing panel, reply card) straight?

Getting It Printed

Once you've made your proofreading and other changes to the layout, you're ready to select your paper. You can use:

❑ your letterhead (if you've used the file *letter.doc*)
❑ white copier paper
❑ colored and/or textured paper

Different types, weights, colors and finishes of paper will give your newsletter different looks. Try printing on several different types and see which will be easiest to read. Which gives you the look you want? Which is heavy enough to withstand being mailed without an envelope (if using one of the self-mailers)? Which papers run well through your copier or laser printer?

Save money on your printing or photocopying by purchasing your paper from a wholesaler. Look for paper distributors in the Yellow

Pages under "Paper Suppliers." Most metropolitan areas have several and most of the distributors will sell to the public.

Finding a Printer

If you're printing 100 copies or less, use your in-house photocopier or laser printer. If you're mailing the newsletter, fold them with the mailing area facing out or put them in an envelope and go to "Getting it Mailed" on page 83. If you're handing them out, stack 'em up and take 'em away.

If you're printing more than 100, print it at a quick print or copy shop. If you have more than 500, find a commercial printing company.

Photocopy service. For simple designs, you can use standard photocopying machines to duplicate your newsletter onto standard paper or pre-printed letterhead. If your list has only a few hundred names, the quality and price may be just right for you. Some copy services also have printing presses for higher quantity jobs. Also, try to find a copy service that can also mail the newsletters for you.

Since there are usually several in each town, look for one convenient to your office. You can also check the Yellow Pages under "Copying Services."

Commercial printers. When shopping for printing, collect quotes from several different printers. Printing prices vary greatly. Get your printer involved in ways you can save money. Ask about the most economical papers to use. Ask if the printer has leftover paper that you can buy at a good price. Get a guarantee on the turnaround time for your job. Try to find a printer who can also mail the newsletters for you.

Some printers can also sort and mail the newsletters. Often, the automated mailing equipment saves you in postage enough to cover the printing expense.

To find printers, seek the referral of another newsletter editor, mailing service, advertising agency or local business. You can also look in the Yellow Pages under "Printers."

Provide clear, written instructions. Your printer will not know your wishes unless clear instructions are given. Specify the color, weight, size and brand of paper you want. Provide written instructions for the number of copies you want. Use the worksheet on page 82 to give your printer the specifications for the job.

Tip:

Many mailing services have printing presses.

Quick Quiz

Before you print your newsletter, take this quiz. (Hint: The answers should all be "yes.")

1. Does the newsletter name and tagline tell, at a glance, what you provide?

2. Are there three to five articles on each page?

3. Is something about your organization on each page?

4. Is there at least one helpful tip for readers on each page?

5. Does everything in the newsletter have some tie back to your product, organization or industry?

Make sure all vital facts are included using **checklstpdf** *on the CD.*

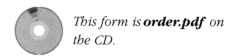 *This form is **order.pdf** on the CD.*

Newsletter Order

Contact: _____

Organization: _____

Address: _____

_____

Phone #: _____

Representative: _____

Printer: _____

Address: _____

_____

Phone #: _____

Job #: _____

Date Due: _____

Payment Terms: _____

Project Name: _____

❏ Sample included

❏ Confirmed price: _____

❏ Quantity: _____

❏ Paper size: ❏ 8 ½ x 11   ❏ 8 ½ x 14   ❏ 11x17   ❏ other:_____

❏ # Pages: ❏ front only   ❏ front & back   ❏ 4-page   ❏ ____ pages

❏ Fold   fold ____ times down to _____ (dimensions)

❏ Perforations: ____ as marked on mark up copy

❏ Paper: ❏ weight:____ ❏ name:_____ ❏ color:_____ ❏ finish:_____

❏ Ink Color: ❏ black   ❏ PMS #_____   ❏ PMS#_____   ❏ other: _____

❏ Photos: ❏ scanned in   ❏ need ____ halftones

❏ Screens: ❏ on artwork   ❏ need _____ cut

❏ Artwork: ❏ paper printout   ❏ on disk, program is _____ version _____

❏ Blue line or other printing proof required

❏ Press check required: Call_____ at _____ when ready for press

❏ Packaging required: ❏ in boxes ready to ship   ❏ shrinkwrapped in ____ s

❏ Shipping: ❏ customer pick up   ❏ deliver to mailhouse at:

      ❏ deliver ____ samples to:

      ❏ deliver ____ samples to address above

      ❏ deliver balance to address above

❏ Ship via: _____

❏ Special instructions:

Getting It Mailed

If you're mailing to a list of 100 or so names and have copied the newsletters yourself, the fastest way to get your newsletter out is to meter or stamp them and send them in today's mail.

If you're short on staff and have more than a few hundred names on your list, find outside help for mailing. A mailing service (also called a "lettershop") affixes labels and postage onto your newsletters, sorts them by zip code and delivers them to the post office.

A good service keeps up with changing regulations and can advise you on the most cost-effective methods of mailing. Find an automated mailing service that can take your database on disk or via modem. They will sort it, remove duplicates, add the ZIP+4 numbers and correct addresses, using data provided by the post office. Then they can print it onto Cheshire (paper) labels or directly onto the newsletter, saving you the cost of pressure-sensitive labels. This frees up your computer's printer and saves you money by preventing you from mailing to outdated addresses.

To find a mailing service, look in the Yellow Pages under "Mailing Services."

Final Steps for Next Time

I hope you've enjoyed our afternoon together. Once your newsletter is out the door, take a moment to make the production of your next newsletter so fast it'll break the sound barrier.

When will the next newsletter need to come out? Do you have any ideas for future newsletters crossed your mind while you were working on this project? What new products, services and events are planned for the next 12 months? Jot them down now. Then, set up your system for collecting your ideas between now and the next issue.

Tips for Staying Organized

Most people are either filers, pilers or tilers. Read on to see which one you are.

Filers. Great files or notes are essential to saving time on future issues. Once you put together your first newsletter, look at the categories you've chosen. Start jotting notes when ideas flash into your mind between issues. File your notes under the issue date (April Newsletter) or the section (Future News Items, Future Who's News, Future Trivia and so on).

Make follow-up to contributors easy by using **followup.pdf** *on the CD.*

Improve your newsletter with each issue by using **updates.pdf** *on the CD.*

Follow-up Checklist

The day after your newsletter is mailed, take a moment to:

❏ Send sample issues to all contributors with thank you notes.

❏ Make sure all customer service representatives in your company have copies of your newsletter before your customers do.

❏ Follow-up on all reader inquiries immediately.

❏ File a sample of the newsletter in your portfolio.

❏ If appropriate, send your newsletter to the local meda and/or trade press that serves your industry.

Avoid Burnout

The constant deadlines and creative demands on editors create an environment prone to burnout. To avoid burnout:

❏ Stay informed

❏ Keep up with technology

❏ Network with other editors

❏ Make sure your writing contains a part of you

❏ Share newsletter talents with family and friends

❏ Donate talents to charities and causes

❏ Set your own standards

❏ Celebrate your success

This filing system may be on paper (usually the easiest—especially for items containing the best ideas—usually Post-its and napkins).

In addition to your idea file, tap into the existing information other people have already researched and edited. Search industry magazines, journals, and newsletter to get ideas. Clip or photocopy the articles and put them into your idea file.

If you're not a "filer," here are a few ideas for "pilers" and "tilers."

Pilers. Set up a box or drawer to pile your newsletter notes and ideas into.

Tilers. If you have a day planner or wall or desk calendar, make notes on these pages or "tiles" as they come up. When you sit down to do the newsletter, go back through the tiles and collect your ideas.

Make News Collection Easy

If you're a bit tired of newsletters at this moment, that's normal. The important thing is to save the work you've done so far in a way that makes the next newsletter easier. And the one after that even easier, yet. Before you know it, you'll be able to put together your newsletter in a fraction of the time it took you today.

Pre-Opened Mail: Postcards

estimated time: 45 minutes

Printed newsletters are great at combatting the out of sight, out of mind syndrome. One of the quickest and easiest ways to stay in front of readers is with a postcard.

Postcard newsletters work to:

- ❑ summarize all of your important news (see *smcardft.pub*)
- ❑ remind people of upcoming events (see *lgcalcd.pub*)
- ❑ draw people to your Web site (see *webcard.pub*)
- ❑ encourage people to sign up for e-mail newsletters (see *permissn.pub*)
- ❑ notify readers that your next newsletter has been published on your Web site and draw them there with teasers (see *rdyonWeb.pub*)

For some applications, they may work better than their longer counterparts because:

- ❑ they're friendly
- ❑ they arrive "pre-opened"
- ❑ they can easily be posted to refrigerators and bulletin boards
- ❑ other people will read them and not feel guilty that they're reading someone else's mail
- ❑ they're less expensive to print and post making it easier to mail more frequently
- ❑ people identify postcards with quick notes from friends

IN THIS CHAPTER:
- ➤ Choose the size of postcard that's right for you
- ➤ Set up your postcard newsletter

Using the Postcard Newsletter Files

The postcard templates on the CD are designed to be used with MS-Publisher. You could also adapt the postcard concept and create your own templates in any other layout program that you use.

Versions of the *webcard* and *smcard* are included for MS-Word. The challenge of using MS-Word for postcards is that you'll need to print out and paste the newsletters 4-up for final copying or printing.

Just Arrived? If you came straight here, please note that you'll need to skim pages 25 to 64 so that the rest of this chapter will make sense.

Note:

When you mail postcards via first class mail, address corrections are free. However, if you mail via bulk mail, you will have to pay for address corrections. If you don't want this service, remove the line, "Address Correction Requested" from the area under your return address.

First Class Postage Rates for Postcards

The *smcard* and *webcard* files are set up to mail first class at 20¢. The *lgcard* files mail at 34¢.

US Postal Regulations for Postcards:

For more information on mailing regulations for postcards, go to: http://new.usps.com/cgi-bin/uspsbv/scripts/content.jsp?D=17527&X=&B=mailing101

Follow the prompts for content in Step 3, pages 25 to 64, to fill in your news. Because of the shorter format, your stories will be brief and only include a few key facts. Be sure to include an action item at the end of all briefs (see page 29, for how to write action lines).

This association newsletter example uses modifications of the files *lgcardft.pub* and *lgcalbk.pub*. It is printed onto Apollo jumbo postcards from PaperDirect.

Printing Multiple Copies Per Page

The MS-Publisher postcard files are set up so that you can print multiple copies per sheet for your final production. When you select Print, click on the button Page Options. When the second window opens, select Print Multiple Copies Per Sheet.

Note:

Consider printing your newsletter on one of the many pre-printed postcard papers available from PaperDirect.

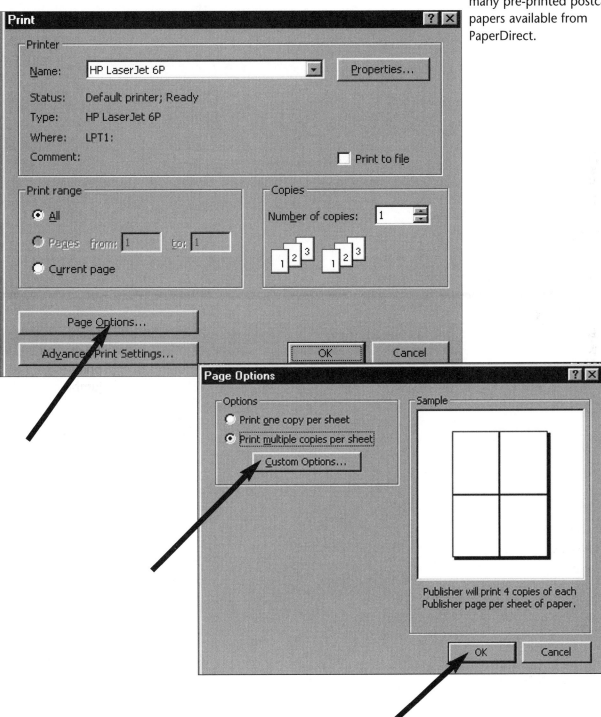

This is an example of a class calendar for a scrapbook store. It is created using the file *lgcalcd.pub*. As the class information was filled in, the card expanded in depth. I moved down the card title and moved the store name and contact name to the empty squares at the bottom (because of the way the dates of June 2003 ran). I filled this box with white to cover the lines of the calendar.

WHAT'S HAPPENING IN [MONTH]

Your Organization's Name
(Your) Phone Number *Call for updates!*
your.email@host.com   www.webadress.com

SUNDAY	MONDAY	TUESDAY	WEDNESDAY	THURSDAY	FRIDAY	SATURDAY
## CLASS NAME/ EVENT Time to Time a.m./p.m. Reservations required?	## CLASS NAME/ EVENT Time to Time a.m./p.m. Reservations required?	## NEWS HEADLINE list reminders, tips, child and new products if no class is happening this day.	## CLASS NAME/ EVENT Time to Time a.m./p.m. Reservations required?	## CLASS NAME/ EVENT Time to Time a.m./p.m. Reservations required?	## CLASS NAME/ EVENT Time to Time a.m./p.m. Reservations required?	## NEWS HEADLINE list reminders, tips, child and new products if no class is happening this day.
## NEWS HEADLINE list reminders, tips, child and new products if no class is happening this day.	## CLASS NAME/ EVENT Time to Time a.m./p.m. Reservations required?	## CLASS NAME/ EVENT Time to Time a.m./p.m. Reservations required?	## CLASS NAME/ EVENT Time to Time a.m./p.m. Reservations required?	## NEWS HEADLINE list reminders, tips, child and new products if no class is happening this day.	## CLASS NAME/ EVENT Time to Time a.m./p.m. Reservations required?	## CLASS NAME/ EVENT Time to Time a.m./p.m. Reservations required?
## CLASS NAME/ EVENT Time to Time a.m./p.m. Reservations required?	## NEWS HEADLINE list reminders, tips, child and new products if no class is happening this day.	## CLASS NAME/ EVENT Time to Time a.m./p.m. Reservations required?	## NEWS HEADLINE list reminders, tips, child and new products if no class is happening this day.	## CLASS NAME/ EVENT Time to Time a.m./p.m. Reservations required?	## NEWS HEADLINE list reminders, tips, child and new products if no class is happening this day.	## CLASS NAME/ EVENT Time to Time a.m./p.m. Reservations required?
## CLASS NAME/ EVENT Time to Time a.m./p.m. Reservations required?	## CLASS NAME/ EVENT Time to Time a.m./p.m. Reservations required?	## CLASS NAME/ EVENT Time to Time a.m./p.m. Reservations required?	## NEWS HEADLINE list reminders, tips, child and new products if no class is happening this day.	## CLASS NAME/ EVENT Time to Time a.m./p.m. Reservations required?	## CLASS NAME/ EVENT Time to Time a.m./p.m. Reservations required?	## NEWS HEADLINE list reminders, tips, child and new products if no class is happening this day.
## NEWS HEADLINE list reminders, tips, child and new products if no class is happening this day.	## CLASS NAME/ EVENT Time to Time a.m./p.m. Reservations required?	## CLASS NAME/ EVENT Time to Time a.m./p.m. Reservations required?	## NEWS HEADLINE list reminders, tips, child and new products if no class is happening this day.	## CLASS NAME/ EVENT Time to Time a.m./p.m. Reservations required?	## NEWS HEADLINE list reminders, tips, child and new products if no class is happening this day.	## CLASS NAME/ EVENT Time to Time a.m./p.m. Reservations required?

SCRAPBOOKING CLASSES, JUNE 2003

SUNDAY	MONDAY	TUESDAY	WEDNESDAY	THURSDAY	FRIDAY	SATURDAY
1 FAMILY DAY Store is closed. Do something special … and take lots of pictures.	**2** MAGAZINES ARRIVE Stop by to pick up the latest issues and ideas	**3**	**4** SUMMER BORDERS CLASS 7 TO 9 p.m. $12; RSVP 555-1212	**5**	**6** CROP AND SHOP 7 TO 9 p.m. $5 (bring a friend for FREE)	**7** TEACHER SALE Great prices on super teacher gifts for the end of the school year.
8 FAMILY DAY Store is closed. Do something special … and take lots of pictures.	**9**	**10** CELEBRATE DADS 15% off on papers and products for Father's Day pages.	**11** MAKING GIFT SCRAPBOOKS 7 TO 9 p.m. $12; RSVP 555-1212	**12** HAPPY HOUR Elaine's famous chocolate cookies are in the classroom. 4 to 5 p.m.	**13** CROP AND SHOP 7 TO 9 p.m. $5 (bring a friend for FREE)	**14** TEACH A FRIEND TO SCRAPBOOK Noon to 4 p.m. All of our class supplies will be out for your use.
15 FAMILY DAY Store is closed. Do something special … and take lots of pictures.	**16** BLUE MONDAY Buy one sheet of blue card stock and get one free!	**17** MARION'S BIRTHDAY Tell her "Happy birth- day" and see what happens.	**18** MAKING MINI SCRAPBOOKS 7 TO 9 p.m. $12; RSVP 555-1212	**19**	**20** CROP AND SHOP 7 TO 9 p.m. $5 (bring a friend for FREE)	**21** ANNIVERSARY SALE! Celebrate our 5th with great savings.
22 FAMILY DAY Store is closed. Do something special … and take lots of pictures.?	**23**	**24** PUNCH ART Save 15% on our new shipment of summer punches.	**25** WEDDING SCRAPBOOKS 7 TO 9 p.m. $12; RSVP 555-1212	**26** HAPPY HOUR Marion mixes up her famous margarita punch (non-alcoholic version available, too)	**27** CROP AND SHOP 7 TO 9 p.m. $5 (bring a friend for FREE)	**28** CUTTING BOARD As we prepare for our next business year, please stop by and give us your feedback. Surprise gift for all.
29 FAMILY DAY Store is closed. Do something special … and take lots of pictures.	**30** GET READY FOR THE 4TH Save 10% on all red, white and blue paper.	**Scrapbooking Memories** Where every memory is a special memory (800) 555-1212 *Call for updates!* elaine@scrapbookmemories.com www.scrapbookmemories.com				

Note:

See the example of the Web site card on page 6.

Fax, E-Mail & Web Site News

NEWS TOOLS

estimated time: 90 minutes

Before you jump into using fax, e-mail or Web sites for newsletters, take a moment to consider your options. First, look at your audience (the checklist on the next page will guide you). The primary question you'll want to answer is, "How do my readers want to receive information?" The answer often varies from reader to reader. You may end up with a plan that includes a mixture of media—sending printed newsletters, faxing special announcements and sending reminders via e-mail.

IN THIS CHAPTER:
- ➤ Choose the new media that's right for you
- ➤ Set up a fax newsletter
- ➤ Create an e-mail newsletter
- ➤ Repurpose your newsletter on the Web

Which New Media Is Right For You?

Many publishers distribute news via new media to save money. The savings on postage and printing are considerable. Another question to consider, though, is "Do your readers need the information fast?" and "Will they see the benefit of the new format over print?"

Graphic abilities or inabilities are another consideration. If you switch a newsletter from print to e-mail, you can no longer include graphics. But if you switch a print newsletter to the Web, you can publish full-color photos.

If your publication is a subscription newsletter (i.e. readers pay to receive it), your circulation will drop if you move it to the Web. Approach e-mail with caution. Consider fax.

> Another good argument against further mega-mergers in the communications industry:
>
> Hi, Phil! I'm the vinyl siding telemarketer you hung up on two minutes ago!

Your Level of Expertise

Up until this point, we've talked about your readers and your content. What about you? Where is your skill level with technology? What shape are your databases in? If you haven't collected e-mail addresses and fax numbers on your readers, the only new media option you can use today is the Web. But the Web requires some resources and expenses, too.

Ah, technology. Turn the page and see how you can use the same quick and easy approach you've seen throughout this book for fax, e-mail and Web site news.

Just Arrived? **STOP**
If you came straight here, please note that you'll need to skim pages 31 through 52 so that the rest of this chapter will make sense.

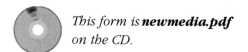

Checklist: Select the Right Media

 The more times you respond "yes" to questions in each of the media, the better your chances are for success in distributing your news using that method.

Fax:

Do you have readers' fax numbers in your database?	❑ yes	❑ no
Will your readers want to save (archive) it?	❑ yes	❑ no
Do readers pay to receive your newsletter?	❑ yes	❑ no
Do your readers prefer being contacted by fax?	❑ yes	❑ no
Are your readers near a fax machine?	❑ yes	❑ no
Do you need to show graphics?	❑ yes	❑ no

E-Mail:

Do you have readers' e-mail addresses in your database?	❑ yes	❑ no
Do your readers prefer being contacted by e-mail?	❑ yes	❑ no
Do your readers check their e-mail every day?	❑ yes	❑ no
Do you have staff to answer responses from readers?	❑ yes	❑ no
Will your readers pass it along (forward it) to others?	❑ yes	❑ no

Web Sites:

Do you currently have a Web site?	❑ yes	❑ no
Do your readers regularly go online?	❑ yes	❑ no
Do the majority have high-speed Internet connections?	❑ yes	❑ no
Do you have a product that few people in the world provide?	❑ yes	❑ no
Do you currently have international readers?	❑ yes	❑ no
Do you need to show graphics in color?	❑ yes	❑ no
Can you easily and inexpensively make changes to your site?	❑ yes	❑ no

How will you lure people to your site to see the newsletter:

- ❑ through an e-mail teaser or summary
- ❑ announcements on postcards
- ❑ faxed announcements
- ❑ mention in print newsletter

Fabulous Fax Newsletters

Postage and printing comprise the lion's share of your out-of-pocket newsletter expenses. What if you could reduce both simultaneously? The solution is fax broadcasting.

Faxes are more visible and immediate than mail. Subjects that lend themselves well to faxing include financial newsletters, stock market and other trend letters, and publications reporting on price increases and decreases. To your readers, a faxed newsletter conveys the image that you're on top of the latest news.

Fax is the only true instant, physical delivery of your news. You can send your newsletter over the phone line and have it delivered to all of your readers on the same day. (E-mail messages and Web pages depend on the recipient to either click "Read" or go to them.) If your readership is local, you even eliminate long distance costs.

Faxed newsletters are used frequently by:

- ❑ associations for membership and meeting news
- ❑ short newsletters
- ❑ text-only newsletters
- ❑ newsletters with timely information
- ❑ subscription (paid) newsletters

For smaller lists, you can distribute the newsletter yourself using WinFax for Windows platforms and Fax stf for Macintosh. The most reliable software to use is that which is included with your modem. When setting up your reader database, include a field for the fax number. This field should be separate from the phone number.

To write and design your fax newsletter, open the file called faxnews. Set up your newsletter name and tagline following the guidelines in Step 2, page 19. Answer the news-generating questions on the screen following the ideas in Step 3, page 25. Fine-tune the writing using the worksheets in Step 4, page 65. Then distribute using the directions in your fax software or those provided by your fax distribution service.

Stay Out of Trouble

It is illegal to send unsolicited faxes. Let people know when you request their fax number that you're setting up your database in a way that allows you to fax them special announcements and other valuable news.

MS-Word: *faxnews.doc*
WordPerfect: *faxnews.wpd*

This nameplate uses the clip art image in the art directory on the disk called faxnews.pcx.

MS-Word:

e-mail-1.doc

e-mail2.doc

WordPerfect:

e-mail1.wpd

e-mail2.wpd

MS-Works:

e-mail1.wps

e-mail2.wps

Easy Retrieval

Name your newsletter in a way that readers can save it into a directory or file and be able to see the issues listed by date. This is done by listing the subject line as the newsletter name followed by the date in the format:

Year-Month-Day

Example:
Newsletter News 03-01-15
Or,
Newsletter News 03-01
(for a monthly)

E-Mail: The Ultimate Quick & Easy Newsletters

E-mail is another low-cost way to distribute news locally, nationally and internationally. If the majority of your customers, employees, members or supporters are online, actively read and reply to e-mail and you have their e-mail addresses, you're halfway there.

E-mail newsletters work great for:

- ❏ associations
- ❏ families
- ❏ small to large customer lists
- ❏ friends and colleagues
- ❏ grassroots activism

To write and design your e-mail newsletter, open up the file e-mail1 or e-mail2 (see the next two pages to choose which design you like). You will use this file to create your newsletter text in your word processor, then copy and paste it into your e-mail program.

First, name your newsletter and give it a tagline using the tips in Step 2, page 19. Use the content questions listed Step 3, page 25, for your type of publication. Fine-tune your headlines and writing using the ideas in Step 4, page 65.

Write in the same friendly tone you use when sending regular e-mail messages or personalized notes. Once you're finished writing, list the headlines of the articles you've written in the contents box (the area that says "Read On For") at the beginning of the newsletter.

Read the instructions for your e-mail program to learn how to distribute your newsletter to more than one address at the same time. Make sure to set your list up such that the entire distribution list doesn't show at the top of your newsletter (test it with your friends first—many a well-meaning publisher has had huge grief over this).

Talk with your Web service provider about setting up an automated list for you, called a majordomo list. Also, see yahoo.com for inforamtion on setting up a group.

Subj:	The News: e news software; contest winners

E-mail readers decide whether or not to read your newsletter in the readers with key words telling them what's inside

```
Month/Year

============ > [NEWSLETTER NAME] < ============

[Subject] tips and trends for [intended audience] published by [organization's name]
_____

READ ON FOR:
_____

= [your first news item]
= [ your next news item]
= [your next news item]
= [your trivia question]

_____

WHAT'S NEW?
_____

[SUBJECT OF YOUR NEWS] + [ACTION IT HAS CREATED]
What is the most important thing that has happened since the last newsletter or will happen soon? What do
readers need to know about it? What does it involve? What changes will it cause? What is being said about
it? Why is it important to readers? Why did it happen?
```

Use These Files With Any Program

If you are currently using or plan to use desktop publishing programs such as MS-Publisher, PageMaker or QuarkXPress, you can use this same text file for the e-mail newsletter to create the articles for your page layout. Then, place this text file into your layout.

The e-mail newsletter follows the same format as the printed versions shown earlier in the book. The only difference is the "Read On For:" section listing the newsletter's contents.

```
WHO'S NEWS?
_____

[PERSON IN THE NEWS] + [ACTION CREATED]
Who is it about? Why is this person being spotlighted? Why is it important to readers? How has he or she
made a difference? How do readers know this person? How did the subject of the story become involved?
What is important about this person? What else has he or she done? What is the person's background?
What are his or her plans for the future?
When did this person become involved with the story or the organization? Where did the events being
written about occur? Where is the person from? Where did he or she attend school or college?

_____

WHAT'S HAPPENING?
_____

WHAT IS THE NAME OF THE EVENT?
When will it happen?
Where will it happen?
Why is it important to readers?
How to sign up.
```

```
DID YOU KNOW?
_____

HOW TO + [INTENDED ACTION] + [SUBJECT]
What should readers know? What should they do? What is your connection to this issue or information?
What are some facts and opinions that affect readers about this issue? How does the issue affect them?
How will it change them? How will it benefit them? Why is it important? Why should readers act on this
issue or piece of information? When can it be used? Who does it affect? Where can readers go for more
information?
```

At the end (or the beginning) of your e-mail news, include information on how to be added to the list along with contact information on your organization.

```
Q&A
_____

Q:

A:

_____

TO SUBSCRIBE:
_____

(Name of newsletter) is published (monthly, # times a year, etc.) by (your name). It is filled with (type of
content) and designed for (intended readers).
To subscribe or unsubscribe, please send an e-mail message to (your e-mail address).

Publisher: (organization's name)
          address
          city/state/zip
          phone number
Editor: (your name here)

Copyright (year) (name of organization)
```

Keep It Short

E-mail newsletters tend to be too long because there is no incentive (such as increased printing costs) to keep it short. Increase readership by:

❑ including a table of contents telling how the information is stacked in the file

❑ following the rules of good headline writing to encourage further reading

❑ giving your newsletter a name that states a benefit

❑ including an issue number in the newsletter name for easy archiving and retrieval

❑ keeping articles short

❑ from time to time print a master contents list for readers who are archiving

See *e-vent.txt* for a format that's useful for sending out e-mail reminders for events.

See *sumary-e.txt* for a format for sending an e-mail summary of news that links to your Web site.

Month/Year

.... [NEWSLETTER NAME] ....

[Subject] tips and trends for [intended audience] published by [organization's name]

....
READ ON FOR:
....

... [your first news item]
... [your next news item]
... [your next news item]
... [your trivia question]

....
WHAT'S NEW?
....

[SUBJECT OF YOUR NEWS] + [ACTION IT HAS CREATED]
What is the most important thing that has happened since the last newsletter or will happen soon? What do readers need to know about it? What does it involve? What changes will it cause? What is being said about it? Why is it important to readers? Why did it happen?

The design of e-mail2 is "lighter" because periods are used to create dotted lines separating the sections.

....
WHO'S NEWS?
....

[PERSON IN THE NEWS] + [ACTION CREATED]
Who is it about? Why is this person being spotlighted? Why is it important to readers? How has he or she made a difference? How do readers know this person? How did the subject of the story become involved? What is important about this person? What else has he or she done? What is the person's background? What are his or her plans for the future?
When did this person become involved with the story or the organization? Where did the events being written about occur? Where is the person from? Where did he or she attend school or college?

....
WHAT'S HAPPENING?
....

WHAT IS THE NAME OF THE EVENT?
When will it happen?
Where will it happen?
Why is it important to readers?
How to sign up.
. . . .

....
Q&A
....
Q:

A:

....
TO SUBSCRIBE:
....

(Name of newsletter) is published (monthly, # times a year, etc.) by (your name). It is filled with (type of content) and designed for (intended readers).
To subscribe or unsubscribe, please send an e-mail message to (your e-mail address).

Publisher: (organization's name)
          address
          city/state/zip
          phone number
Editor: (your name here)

Copyright (year) (name of organization)

Web Site Wonders

The Worldwide Web is truly a global news medium. A good site contains news for both your customers and prospects as well as for the press. Web sites are often used as additional places to broadcast your news but rarely as the only place. The drawbacks are that all of your members, customers and prospects must have access to the Web. They must be highly motivated because they're going to have to actively seek out your site.

The benefit of the Web is that you have to upload the new message to only one spot and you can easily include color graphics. Mixed media, such as sending an e-mail teaser that draws people to the Web site or broadcasting a fax that offers a free e-mail newsletter, is an ideal use of all new technologies.

On your Web site, concentrate on excellent news content. Make your site a library of information. Rotate your content frequently. Try changing one section weekly and using tips or cartoons.

When you set up your text, avoid long paragraphs. Break up articles into one or two sentence paragraphs followed by bulleted or numbered lists. Keep your newsletter short and simple. For most audiences, choose good content over fancy graphics. Graphics take longer to upload to readers' screens.

To create your Web site newsletter, open the file webnews.htm using a Web publishing software program.

Next, name your newsletter and give it a tagline using the tips in Step 2, page 19. Use the content questions listed Step 3, page 25. Fine-tune your headlines and writing using the worksheets in Step 4, page 65.

Note: Setting up a managing a Web site is beyond the scope of this book. This section walks you through using the Web newsletter template on the disk. It is intended to help you create a file that you could send to your Web master or Internet provider.

Signing Off...

Regardless of the new media you use and when you use it, continue to watch technological changes that can help keep in touch with your community of readers through news. It's an exciting time to be a news writer and editor.

News on Tape

If you're considering recording your news and distributing it on tape or CD, learn more about the power of audio in the book *Words on Tape*, by Judy Byers.

It shows how to create profitable spoken word audio on cassettes and CDs. The book (list price $27.95) is available by mail from The Tattered Cover Bookstore, Denver, CO; (303) 322-7727.

newmedia / webnews.htm

Combine Web Site Newsletters with Postcards & E-Mail

Use an e-mail summary from *sumary-e.txt* or the postcards *rdyonWeb* or *webcard* to draw traffic to your Web site newsletter.

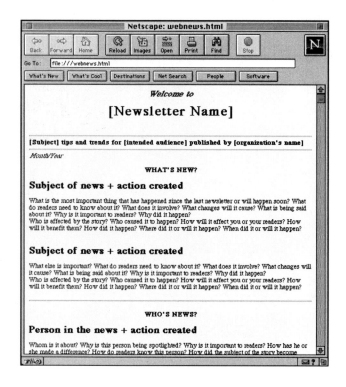

Convert your printed, faxed or e-mail newsletter to Web site news by following the same format you've used throughout the book. The Web is an idea place to reach new prospects with helpful information about your organization.

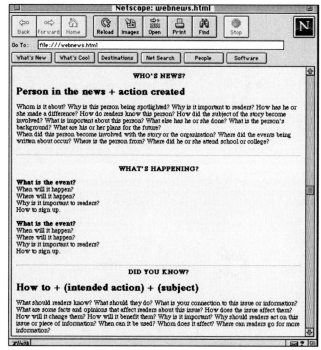

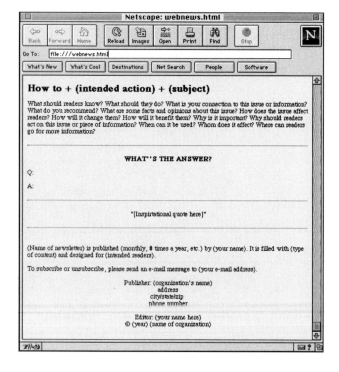

estimated time: 90 minutes

Press Releases

S tudies have shown that editorial mentions outpull advertising in the same media by anywhere from three to 16 times.

Similar to the news that you publish, media relations serve to educate and inform the public, position your organization, improve morale and move along sales. Often, a press release will result in a full feature story about your organization or your products, services or causes.

10 Tips for Getting Great Media Coverage

Here are some tips for working with the media.

1. Send your news release only to publications that print similar news. Read the publication and get a feel for the common writing style. Write your press release using the same style.

2. Write your news release in a way that makes it newsworthy—it must include as many of the following as possible: timely, of a local angle, unusual, never heard before, controversial, involving many people or including a VIP.

3. Include an eye-catching photograph. Include a caption for the photo—type the information and tape it to the back so that the caption sticks out from under the photo. Fold the paper against the photo to protect it during mailing. In the caption, include the names of the people in the photo and other information on the setting or event. Use the present tense when describing any action.

4. If you want to reach radio stations, include suggestions for interviewing (include a list of questions or "talking points"). If there are other interesting sounds, for radio, or sounds and sights, for television, list those ideas at the end of the release or in a cover letter. For radio stations, suggest trivia questions with prizes that you provide during an interview with a member of your organization.

IN THIS CHAPTER:
- ➤ Broadcasting your news in many other places
- ➤ Do's and don'ts of working with the media
- ➤ Sending out a top 10 list

Note:

Some organizations who have had trouble getting local media attention have good luck when hiring a local publicist.

Note:

Keep current of news. Send letters to the editor with add-on comments to stories that have already run. Provide local angles to national news and expert opinion to general news stories that touch your specialty.

Sources for Media Lists

Print, Radio & TV:
Bradley Communications
Landsdowne, PA
(610) 259-0707

Print, Radio & TV:
Bacons Media Checker
Chicago, IL
(312) 922-2400

Magazines:
Standard Rates & Data
You can find this at most libraries

Subscription Newsletters:
Hudson's Newsletter Directory
(914) 876-2081

Subscription Newsletters:
Gale Research Newsletters
Directory
(313) 961-2242

Subscription Newsletters:
Oxbridge Directory of
Newsletters
(212) 741-0231

Specialty Cable Stations:
Literary MarketPlace
Available at most libraries

Newspapers:
Working Press of the Nation
Available at most libraries

*Links to the Web sites of many
media organizations:*
Gebbie Press
www.gebbieinc.com

*To send out your event
news, see* **pressrel.doc**
on the CD.

5. Mail or e-mail your release but do not fax it unless specifically requested to by the editor.

6. Keep a list of the top three points you want to make during an interview. After you send out your news release, keep this list near your phone is case a reporter calls.

7. Give all press inquiries top priority. Return calls right away. Find out when the reporter's deadline is and strive to help meet it.

8. Provide other resources that will help the editor write or produce the story. Note: These resources may not benefit your organization in any way but will make it likely that you will be called again as a resource.

9. Send all promised follow-up information right away. Request to fact-check your part of the story. Explain that you will be looking only at the technical facts for accuracy. Many reporters won't let you but it won't hurt to ask.

10. Send a thank you note after the story is printed. Be gracious if there were any errors in the story (it happens to us all).

No News? Make a Top 10 List

The Top 10 List format is also a great way to generate media mentions when you don't have any current news to release. Your Top 10 list will most likely have an educational angle. Use any of the questions from Step 3 in the education section of each of the types of newsletters (sales, association, non-profit and community) as prompts.

For example, the text from above could be converted to a Top 10 format and sent out to business magazines.

You can also publish this Top 10 list in your own newsletter, Web site and e-mail to keep your NewsWave rolling!

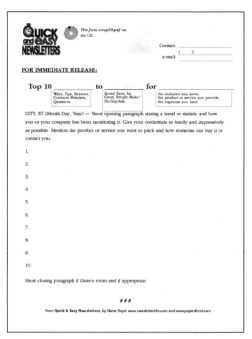

This form is **top10.pdf**
on the CD.

Using MS-Word, WordPerfect & MS-Works

estimated time: 20 minutes

Welcome to the MS-Word, WordPerfect and MS-Works Help Files of *Quick & Easy Newsletters.* These files contain the fastest, most effective way I know to get the good news from your organization into the hands of your readers—in a format they'll love.

Read No Further...

These files are designed with busy people in mind—this section contains the essentials you need to jump right in. Refer to the rest as you put together each section of your newsletter. The pointing finger will guide you along.

The files set up on the disk are not templates or wizards. They are documents just like you've created when you've set up letters or reports. The best way to explain is to give you a quick tour right on your own computer. Put the CD into your disk drive and turn to the page covering the software you use:

MS-WORD 👉 page 101

WORDPERFECT 👉 page 108

MS-WORKS 👉 page 115

System Requirements:

MS-Word, version 6.0 and higher

WordPerfect, version 6.0 and higher

MS-Works, version 3.0 and higher

Windows 3.1 and **Windows 95** and higher.

Macintosh platforms with PC Exchange drives and running software listed above.

One of the joys of installing new software.

Note:

If you have a computer with preloaded or bundled software from Microsoft and have not purchased MS-Word or WordPerfect separately, you probably have MS-Works.

Note:

The screens on the following pages show the disk in the a: drive. This updated kit has the files on a CD so you will probably see the disk on your m: or n: drive.

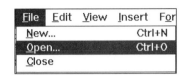

Fire Up MS-Word

After Word is open on your screen, take a test drive of the files by opening the Word document **2c-lettr** that's in the Word directory on the CD.

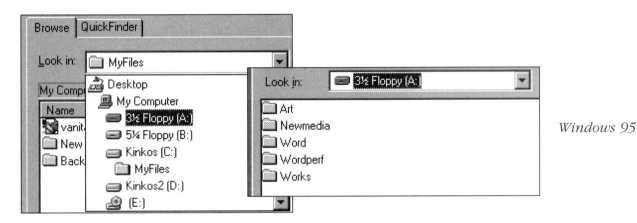

Windows 95

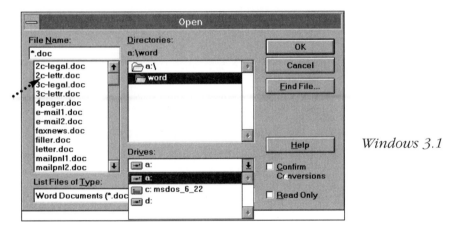

Windows 3.1

The gray bars, What's Happening and What's News, may line up across your screen or they may have shifted. Because of differences in printer and software set-ups, what you see on the screen may look different. No problem. It gives us a great chance to start working with the document.

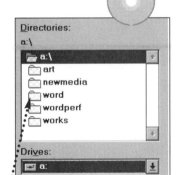

What's on the CD?

Word users will find the design files in the directory word.

A printout of the clip art, cartoons and other filler that's on the CD is in the Appendix, "What's on the CD?" on page 129.

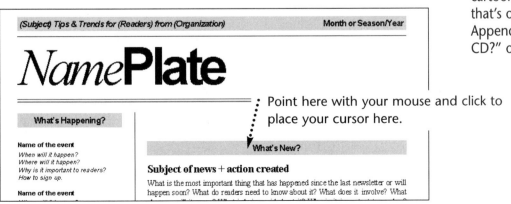

Point here with your mouse and click to place your cursor here.

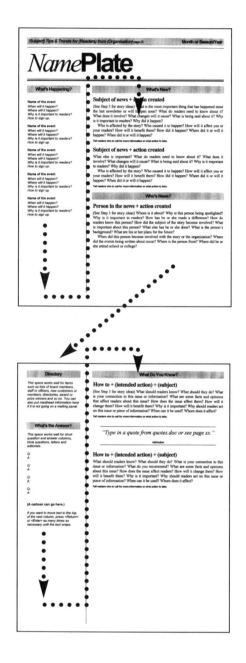

How to Move Text Where You Want It

If your screen looks like the one at the bottom of the previous page, place the cursor before the "W" in "What's News" in the gray bar and press the Backspace key on your keyboard until it lines up with "What's Happening."

If your screen looks like the example directly below, scroll down to the bottom of the page.

Place your cursor in the blank line directly about "What's New?" and press Return or Enter until you no longer see "What's New?" If you scroll back to the top of the page, you will now see it at the top of the second column.

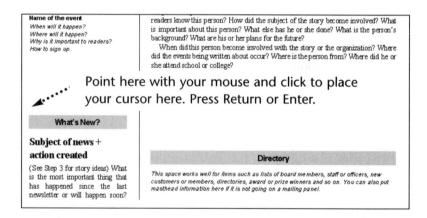

This is how you will move your articles from column to column and page to page throughout any of the design files on the disk. Scroll on down through the document and move some other text around. **Get comfortable with the way the text moves before you start any writing.**

Back-up, Save and Undo

Setting up a newsletter in software designed for word processing can get tricky. As you're typing in your news, text will move around on the screen. Most of it you can ignore and fix later. But, to avoid primal screaming, do these three steps now:

1. Make a back-up copy of the CD.
2. Set up MS-Word to make automatic backups.

Saving & Undoing

When things are going right:

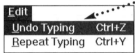

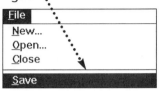

If something goes wrong:

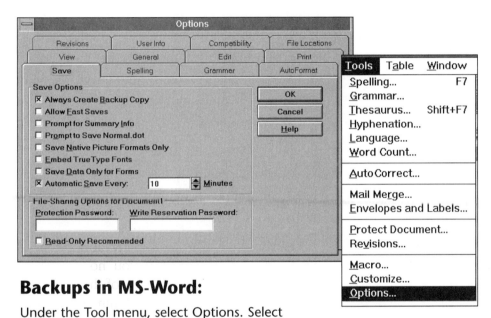

Backups in MS-Word:

Under the Tool menu, select Options. Select the box for "Always Create Backup Copy" and "Automatic Save Every." The backup file will be saved in the same place as the original file with the extension ".bak."

Save

Save your work to your hard drive (or wherever you usually save your work). To avoid accidentally over-writing your work, give your files different names than the ones that are on the CD.

In MS-Word, you can undo multiple operations when the Standard toolbar is showing.

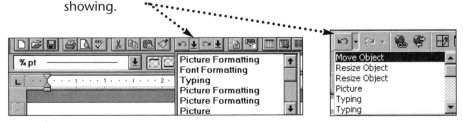

Windows 3.1

Windows 95

A Quick Look at How You'll Use These Designs

Scroll back up to the top of page one on your screen. You've probably already noticed the questions on the screen. These questions are designed so that, when you answer them, you automatically build a newsletter article. Go ahead and give it a quick try here.

Place your cursor at the end of "When did it or will it happen?" and press Return or Enter. You'll see your cursor flashing in a new line as shown below.

Ignore the headline (Subject of news...) for now and start by answering the first question, "What is the most important thing that has happened since the last newsletter?" Continue through all of the other questions and answer those that apply (ignore those that don't).

Help With the Blinking Cursor Syndrome

If you're stuck on what to write about, just make up something for practice. Step 3, page 25, will help give you ideas for news stories. In addition, the planning you'll do in Step 1 will guide you in basic decisions about what to include.

What's Happening?

Name of the event
When will it happen?
Where will it happen?
Why is it important to readers?
How to sign up.

What's New?

Subject of news + action created

What is the most important thing that has happened since the last newsletter or will happen soon? What do readers need to know about it? What does it involve? What changes will it cause? What is being said about it? Why is it important to readers? Why did it happen?

Who is affected by the story? Who caused it to happen? How will it affect you or your readers? How will it benefit them? How did it happen? Where did it or will it happen? When did it or will it happen?

Tell readers who to call for more information or what action to take.

Place your cursor at the end of the second paragraph and press return. This holds the font and size from the previous paragraph. Answer the questions above the cursor to create a sample news article.

What's New?

Subject of news + action created

What is the most important thing that has happened since the last newsletter or will happen soon? What do readers need to know about it? What does it involve? What changes will it cause? What is being said about it? Why is it important to readers? Why did it happen?

Who is affected by the story? Who caused it to happen? How will it affect you or your readers? How will it benefit them? How did it happen? Where did it or will it happen? When did it or will it happen?

Newsletter Resources is releasing a new book called *Quick & Easy Newsletters*. Five years in the making, this book helps people create a newsletter in an afternoon. It's designed for use with MS-Word, WordPerfect and MS-Works. This product was created for those who've wanted to do a newsletter for a long time but didn't have the time or want to learn how to use a desktop publishing program.

Now, anyone with access to a computer and a photocopier can do a newsletter. The book is written by Elaine Floyd with the help of Susan Todd. It will be available at the end of this month through newsletter seminar companies and book stores.

Call (800) 264-6305 for more information on the book.

When you're finished, delete the questions listed above the news article you've written.

What's New?

Subject of news + action created

Newsletter Resources is releasing a new book called *Quick & Easy Newsletters*. Five years in the making, this book helps people create a newsletter in an afternoon. It's designed for use with MS-Word, WordPerfect and MS-Works. This product was created for those who've wanted to do a newsletter for a long time but didn't have the time or want to learn how to use a desktop publishing program.

Now, anyone with access to a computer and a photocopier can do a newsletter. The book is written by Elaine Floyd with the help of Susan Todd. It will be available at the end of this month through newsletter seminar companies and book stores.

Call (800) 264-6305 for more information on the book.

Person in the news + action created

Who is it about? Why is this person being spotlighted? Why is it important to readers? How has he or she made a difference? How do readers know this person? How did the subject of the story become involved? What is important about this person? What else has he or she done? What is the person's background? What are his or her plans for the future?

When did this person become involved with the story or the organization? Where did the events being written about occur? Where is the person from? Where did he or she attend school or college?

Mitchell Financial has been named Nashville Small Business of the year. Rita

Mitchel has been a long-time newsletter publisher and fan of Newsletter Resources products. She has been publishing a newsletter since 1987. Says Rita, "I never would have received the

Note:

When you get down to the Who's News section at the bottom of the page, the text you type in will wrap to the skinny margin on the second page. Let the text go there for now while you write your article. After you're finished—when you remove the questions—it may all fit on the page.

Person in the news + action created

Mitchell Financial has been named Nashville Small Business of the year. Rita Mitchel has been a long-time newsletter publisher and fan of Newsletter Resources products. She has been publishing a newsletter since 1987. Says Rita, "I never would have received the exposure to win this award without my newsletter." In addition to being an avid newsletter publisher, Rita serves on the Small Business Council for the Small Business Administration.

Rita was the first of Newsletter Resources' clients to try the Quick & Easy Newsletter format. She sat in Elaine's office 10 years ago and they discussed the fastest way to do a newsletter. The first Rita's Report came out one week later--a

If the text still wraps, either edit it to fit (as done below) or copy the text that's in the margin and paste it to the second column

simple one-pager photocopied onto Rita's letterhead.

Person in the news + action created

Mitchell Financial has been named Nashville Small Business of the year. Rita Mitchel has been a long-time newsletter publisher and fan of Newsletter Resources products. She has been publishing a newsletter since 1987. Says Rita, "I never would have received the exposure to win this award without my newsletter." In addition to being a newsletter publisher, Rita serves on the Small Business Council for SBA

Rita was the first of Newsletter Resources' clients to try the Quick & Easy Newsletter format. She sat in Elaine's office 10 years ago and they discussed the fastest way to do a newsletter. The first Rita's Report came out one week later--a simple one-pager photocopied onto Rita's letterhead.

being an avid newsletter publisher, Rita serves on the Small Business Counc Small Business Administration.

Rita was the first of Newsletter Resources' clients to try the Quick Newsletter format. She sat in Elaine's office 10 years ago and they discussed

Text edited to fit.

fastest way to do a newsletter. The first Rita's Report came out one week later--a simple one-pager photocopied onto Rita's letterhead.

Text copied and pasted into the second column. This text will shift around as you fill the first column but you can move it back using the Return or Delete keys.

Tip:

For a better feel for what's on the page, print this document and any of the other design documents in the Word directory on the disk. See pages 14 and 15 for recommendations on which designs to use.

Tip:

Experiment with adding clipart to this file now. Follow the instructions for your program listed on page 21.

Using the Style Menus

You can also see the styles under the toolbar.

Styles are pre-formatted fonts set up for your document. The newsletter files on the disks are set up using styles for the text, headlines and other areas of the newsletters.

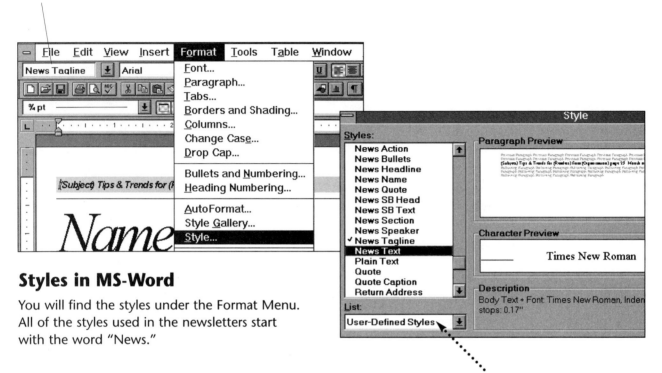

Styles in MS-Word

You will find the styles under the Format Menu. All of the styles used in the newsletters start with the word "News."

In Windows 95 the style toolbar looks like this.

Set up your style menu to show only the User-Defined Styles.

As you type in text on the screen, if it's not in the right style, you can select it and change it using the style menu in Word. To see which styles are used where, see the text in parentheses on page 4.

News copy
(News Text)

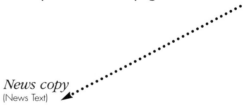

Why Did It Do That?

As you're typing on the screen, some of the fonts may change to styles you don't want. Keep the words you've written, select them and go under the style menu to change them to the style you want.

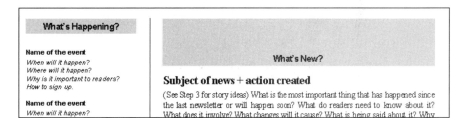

	is it important to readers? Why did it happen?
nt	Who is affected by the story? Who caused it to happen? How will it affect you or
en?	your readers? How will it benefit them? How did it happen? Where did it or will it
en?	happen? When did it or will it happen?
t to readers?	**Tell readers who to call for more information or what**
	action to take.Subject of news + action created
nt	
en?	What else is important? What do readers need to know about it? What does it

To change the text "Tell readers..." back to the small font, place your cursor before the word "Subject" and press Return or Enter. Select the text you want to change and select News Action under the Style menu.

IMPORTANT:

This book is not a replacement for your MS-Word manual, Help screens or technical support. Please refer to those sources with questions that deal with the software's operation.

If you get an expanded gray bar, place the cursor before the W in What's News and press Backspace or place the cursor one line up and press Delete.

What's Happening?	
Name of the event	
When will it happen?	**What's New?**
Where will it happen?	
Why is it important to readers?	**Subject of news + action created**
How to sign up.	(See Step 3 for story ideas) What is the most important thing that has happened since
Name of the event	the last newsletter or will happen soon? What do readers need to know about it?
When will it happen?	What does it involve? What changes will it cause? What is being said about it? Why

Here are a few other tips for Word users:

❑ Make sure you're in Page Layout view (change this under the View menu)

❑ Open the Standard and Formatting toolbars (under the View menu in Toolbars)

❑ Select AutoCorrect under the Tools menu. Word will correct typos as you work. Mark Change Straight Quotes to Smart Quotes.

❑ Adjust the Zoom Control to a comfortable viewing size. Try 75%..

You're **finished with the tour of MS-Word.**

Go to Step 1: Pain-Free Planning

page 7

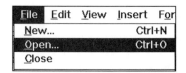

Fire Up WordPerfect

After WordPerfect is open on your screen, take a test drive of the files by opening the WordPerfect document **2c-lettr** that's in the wordperf directory on the CD.

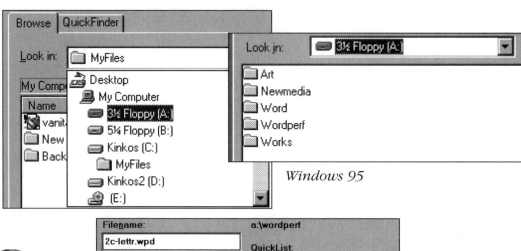

Windows 95

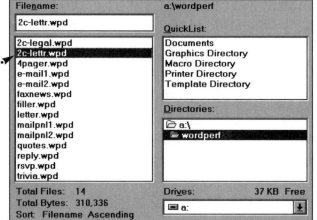

Windows 3.1

What's on the CD?

WordPerfect users will find the design files in the directory wordperf.

A printout of the clip art, cartoons and other filler that's on the CD is in the Appendix, "What's on the CD?" on page 129.

As the file opens, you may get a message saying that the file was formatted on a different printer. That's normal. Once the file is open, the gray bars, What's Happening and What's News, may line up across your screen or they may have shifted. Because of differences in printer and software set-ups, what you see on the screen may look different. No problem. It gives us a great chance to start working with the document.

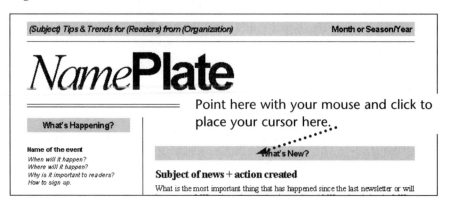

WORDPERFECT

How to Move Text Where You Want It

If your screen looks like the one at the bottom of the previous page, place the cursor before the "W" in "What's News" in the gray bar and press the Backspace key on your keyboard until it lines up with "What's Happening."

If your screen looks like the example directly below, scroll down to the bottom of the page.

Place your cursor in the blank line directly about "What's New?" and press Return or Enter until you no longer see "What's New?" If you scroll back to the top of the page, you will now see it at the top of the second column.

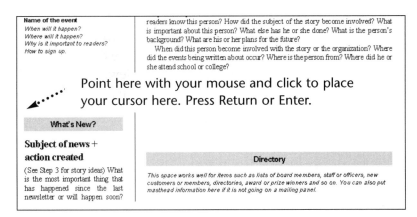

Point here with your mouse and click to place your cursor here. Press Return or Enter.

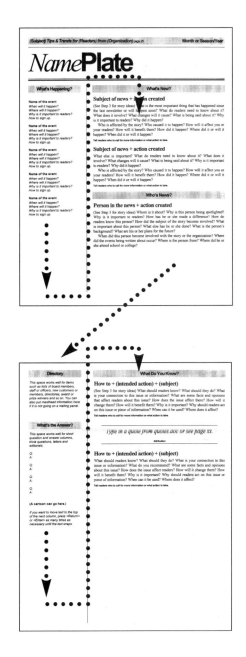

This is how you will move your articles from column to column and page to page throughout any of the design files on the disk. Scroll on down through the document and move some other text around. **Get comfortable with the way the text moves before you start any writing.**

Saving & Undoing

When things are going right:

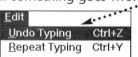

If something goes wrong:

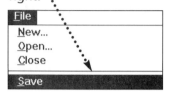

Back-up, Save and Undo

Setting up a newsletter in software designed for word processing can get tricky. As you're typing in your news, text will move around on the screen. Most of it you can ignore and fix later. But, to avoid primal screaming, do these three steps now:

1. Make a back-up copy of the CD.
2. Set up WordPerfect to make automatic backups.

Backups in WordPerfect:

Under the File Menu, select Preferences. Click on the icon for File. Select the box for "Timed Document Backup Every" and "Original Document Backup." The backup file will be saved in the same place as the original file with the extension ".bk!."

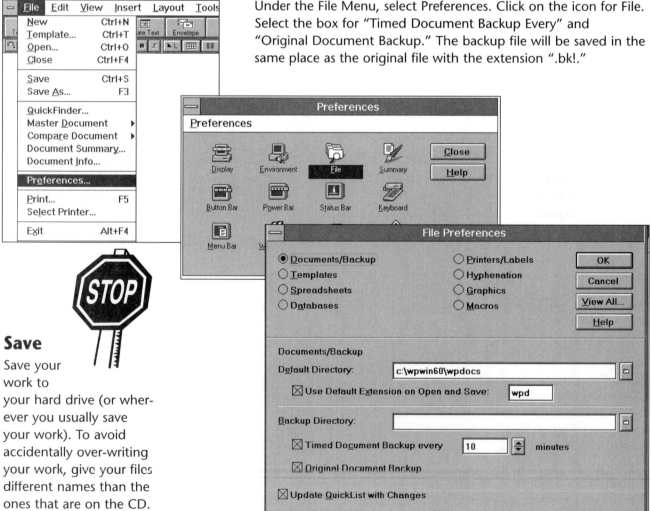

Save

Save your work to your hard drive (or wherever you usually save your work). To avoid accidentally over-writing your work, give your files different names than the ones that are on the CD.

A Quick Look at How You'll Use These Designs

Scroll back up to the top of page one on your screen. You've probably already noticed the questions on the screen. These questions are designed so that, when you answer them, you automatically build a newsletter article. Go ahead and give it a quick try here.

Place your cursor at the end of "When did it or will it happen?" and press Return or Enter. You'll see your cursor flashing in a new line as shown below.

Ignore the headline (Subject of news…) for now and start by answering the first question, "What is the most important thing that has happened since the last newsletter?" Continue through all of the other questions and answer those that apply (ignore those that don't).

Help With the Blinking Cursor Syndrome

If you're stuck on what to write about, just make up something for practice. Step 3, page 25, will help give you ideas for news stories. In addition, the planning you'll do in Step 1 will guide you in basic decisions about what to include.

What's Happening?	What's New?
Name of the event *When will it happen?* *Where will it happen?* *Why is it important to readers?* *How to sign up.* **Name of the event** *When will it happen?* *Where will it happen?* *Why is it important to readers?* *How to sign up.*	**Subject of news + action created** What is the most important thing that has happened since the last newsletter or will happen soon? What do readers need to know about it? What does it involve? What changes will it cause? What is being said about it? Why is it important to readers? Why did it happen? Who is affected by the story? Who caused it to happen? How will it affect you or your readers? How will it benefit them? How did it happen? When did it or will it happen? Tell readers who to call for more information or what action to take.

Place your cursor at the end of the second paragraph and press return. This holds the font and size from the previous paragraph. Answer the questions above the cursor to create a sample news article.

What's New?

Subject of news + action created

What is the most important thing that has happened since the last newsletter or will happen soon? What do readers need to know about it? What does it involve? What changes will it cause? What is being said about it? Why is it important to readers? Why did it happen?

Who is affected by the story? Who caused it to happen? How will it affect you or your readers? How will it benefit them? How did it happen? Where did it or will it happen? When did it or will it happen?

Newsletter Resources is releasing a new book called *Quick & Easy Newsletters*. Five years in the making, this book helps people create a newsletter in an afternoon. It's designed for use with MS-Word, WordPerfect and MS-Works. This product was created for those who've wanted to do a newsletter for a long time but didn't have the time or want to learn how to use a desktop publishing program.

Now, anyone with access to a computer and a photocopier can do a newsletter. The book is written by Elaine Floyd with the help of Susan Todd. It will be available the end of this month through newsletter seminar companies and book stores.

Call (800) 264-6305 for more information on the book.

What's New?

Subject of news + action created

Newsletter Resources is releasing a new book called *Quick & Easy Newsletters*. Five years in the making, this book helps people create a newsletter in an afternoon. It's designed for use with MS-Word, WordPerfect and MS-Works. This product was created for those who've wanted to do a newsletter for a long time but didn't have the time or want to learn how to use a desktop publishing program.

Now, anyone with access to a computer and a photocopier can do a newsletter. The book is written by Elaine Floyd with the help of Susan Todd. It will be available at the end of this month through newsletter seminar companies and book stores.

Call (800) 264-6305 for more information on the book.

When you're finished, delete the questions listed above the news article you've written.

Note:

When you get down to the Who's News section at the bottom of the page, the text you type in will wrap to the skinny margin on the second page. Let the text go there for now while you write your article. After you're finished—when you remove the questions—it may all fit on the page.

Person in the news + action created

Who is it about? Why is this person being spotlighted? Why is it important to readers? How has he or she made a difference? How do readers know this person? How did the subject of the story become involved? What is important about this person? What else has he or she done? What is the person's background? What are his or her plans for the future?

When did this person become involved with the story or the organization? Where did the events being written about occur? Where is the person from? Where did he or she attend school or college?

Mitchell Financial has been named Nashville Small Business of the year. Rita

Mitchel has been a long-time newsletter publisher and fan of Newsletter Resources products. She has been publishing a newsletter since 1987. Says Rita, "I never would have received the

Person in the news + action created

Mitchell Financial has been named Nashville Small Business of the year. Rita Mitchel has been a long-time newsletter publisher and fan of Newsletter Resources products. She has been publishing a newsletter since 1987. Says Rita, "I never would have received the exposure to win this award without my newsletter." In addition to being an avid newsletter publisher, Rita serves on the Small Business Council for the Small Business Administration.

Rita was the first of Newsletter Resources' clients to try the Quick & Easy Newsletter format. She sat in Elaine's office 10 years ago and they discussed the fastest way to do a newsletter. The first Rita's Report came out one week later--a

If the text still wraps, either edit it to fit (as done below) or copy the text that's in the margin and paste it to the second column

simple one-pager photocopied onto Rita's letterhead.

Person in the news + action created

Mitchell Financial has been named Nashville Small Business of the year. Rita Mitchel has been a long-time newsletter publisher and fan of Newsletter Resources products. She has been publishing a newsletter since 1987. Says Rita, "I never would have received the exposure to win this award without my newsletter." In addition to being a newsletter publisher, Rita serves on the Small Business Council for SBA

Rita was the first of Newsletter Resources' clients to try the Quick & Easy Newsletter format. She sat in Elaine's office 10 years ago and they discussed the fastest way to do a newsletter. The first Rita's Report came out one week later--a simple one-pager photocopied onto Rita's letterhead.

Text edited to fit.

being an avid newsletter publisher, Rita serves on the Small Business Counc Small Business Administration.

Rita was the first of Newsletter Resources' clients to try the Quick Newsletter format. She sat in Elaine's office 10 years ago and they discussed

fastest way to do a newsletter. The first Rita's Report came out one week later--a simple one-pager photocopied onto Rita's letterhead.

Tip:

For a better feel for what's on the page, print this document and any of the other design documents in the Word directory on the disk. See pages 14 and 15 for recommendations on which designs to use.

Text copied and pasted into the second column. This text will shift around as you fill the first column but you can move it back using the Return or Delete keys.

Tip:

Experiment with adding clipart to this file now. Follow the instructions for your program listed on page 21.

Using the Style Menus

Styles are pre-formatted fonts set up for your document. The newsletter files on the disks are set up using styles for the text, headlines and other areas of the newsletters.

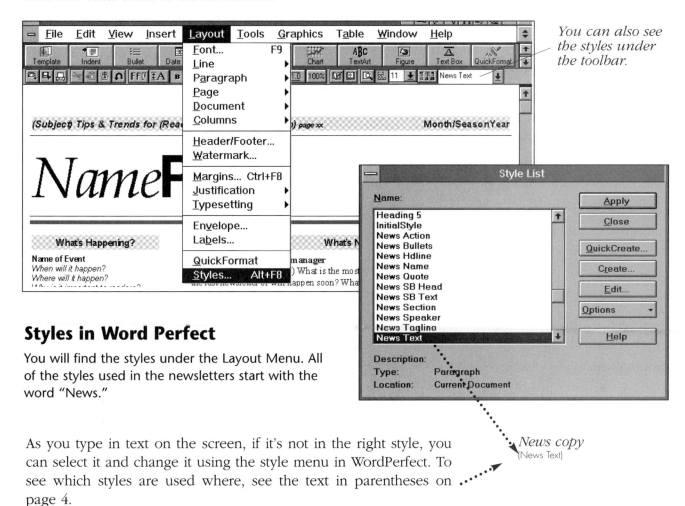

You can also see the styles under the toolbar.

News copy
(News Text)

Styles in Word Perfect

You will find the styles under the Layout Menu. All of the styles used in the newsletters start with the word "News."

As you type in text on the screen, if it's not in the right style, you can select it and change it using the style menu in WordPerfect. To see which styles are used where, see the text in parentheses on page 4.

Stubborn Styles

In some versions of WordPerfect, selecting the styles from the Style menu doesn't override the styles on the screen. If this happens, note the font used in the style and select Font under the Layout menu and reset the font, size and attributes here.

IMPORTANT:

This book is not a replacement for your WordPerfect. manual, Help screens or technical support. Please refer to those sources with questions that deal with the software's operation.

If you get an expanded gray bar, place the cursor before the W in What's News and press Backspace or place the cursor one line up and press Delete.

You're finished with the tour of WordPerfect.

Go to Step 1: Pain-Free Planning:

page 7

Why Did It Do That?

As you're typing on the screen, some of the fonts may change to styles you don't want. Keep the words you've written, select them and go under the style menu to change them to the style you want.

To change the text "Tell readers..." back to the small font, place your cursor before the word "Subject" and press Return or Enter. Select the text you want to change and select News Action under the Style menu.

Here are a few other tips for WordPerfect users:

❑ Sometimes when you copy and paste or even enter new text, the formatting of a line or paragraph will change. The text may become bold or the font size will change. Try selecting the text and reselecting the style using the styles. If that doesn't fix it, select Font under the Layout menu and reset the font, size and attributes.

❑ If an unwanted gray background covers a section of your text, get rid of the gray by going to the Layout menu and selecting Columns. Click on Border/Fill and remove the fill.

❑ When just adding one or two sentences or correcting a line, place the cursor next to text that has font style you want.

❑ If the text is bold and Bold is not depressed on the Power Bar or checked on the Font menu, go to the View menu and select Reveal Codes. Find the incorrect Bold code and remove it by clicking and dragging it from the window.

❑ In the WordPerfect designs, the line between the columns is removed from the design. **Add the line back only after you have finished all writing and designing of your document. In older versions, the lines between columns cause the document to be unstable.**

To add the vertical line, go to the Layout menu and select Columns. Click on Border/Fill and select Column Between on the Border Style window. In WordPerfect 7.0, go under the Graphics menu and select Vertical Line.

Fire Up MS-Works

After MS-Works is open on your screen, take a test drive of the files by opening the document **2c-lettr** that's in the works directory on the CD.

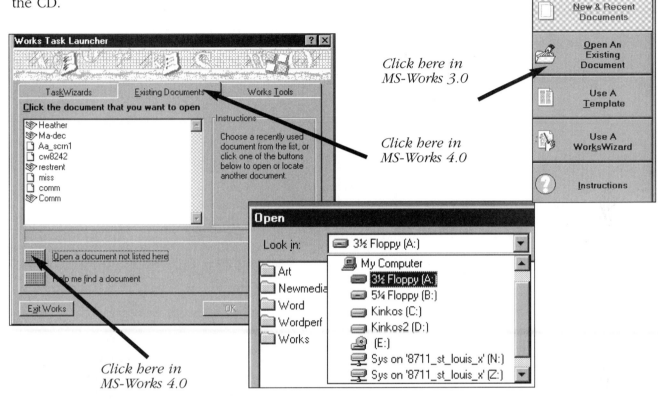

Click here in MS-Works 3.0

Click here in MS-Works 4.0

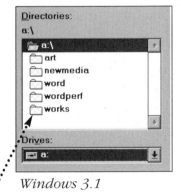

Click here in MS-Works 4.0

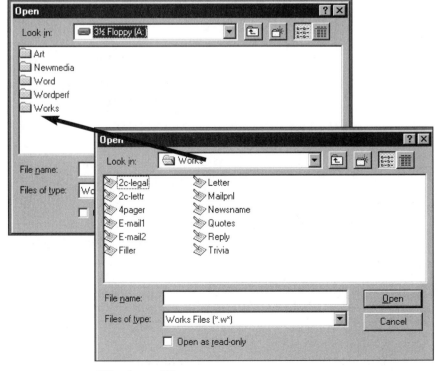

Windows 3.1

What's on the CD?

Works users will find the design files in the directory works.

A printout of the clip art, cartoons and other filler that's on the CD is in the Appendix, "What's on the CD?" on page 129.

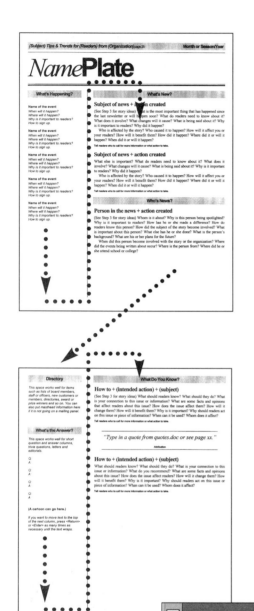

Take a Tour of the Newsletter

With the file 2c-lettr open, take a look. The gray bars, What's Happening and What's News, may line up across your screen or they may have shifted. Because of differences in printer and software set-ups, what you see on the screen may look different. No problem. It gives us a great chance to start working with the document.

To leave room for the nameplate (see page 118), the text in all columns on the first page has been moved down by inserting paragraph returns. The template is set with ten returns before the text starts. If you click on All Characters under the View menu, you can see paragraph symbols (¶). Add returns or take them away to make the gray bars across the top of your screen line up.

Keep in mind that the size of the blank space created by hitting "Enter" varies with type size, so if you have spacing inconsistencies between paragraphs or sections, highlight the paragraph symbol and change the type size.

Scroll through the rest of the file and get a feel for how the newsletter is set up. Print out a copy and take a look, too. Get comfortable with the way the text moves on the screen before you start any writing.

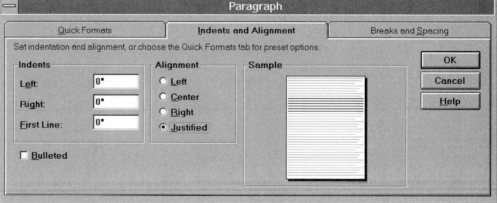

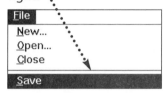
Back-up, Save and Undo

Setting up a newsletter in software designed for word processing can get tricky. As you're typing in your news, text will move around on the screen. Most of it you can ignore and fix later. But, to avoid primal screaming, do these three steps now:

1. Make a back-up copy of the CD.
2. Set up MS-Works to make automatic backups.

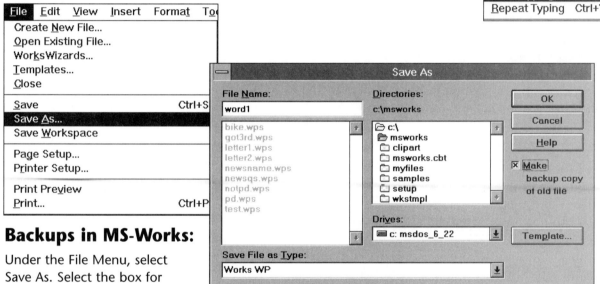

Backups in MS-Works:

Under the File Menu, select Save As. Select the box for "Make backup copy of old file." The backup file will be saved in the same place as the original file with the extension .bk!

Saving & Undoing

When things are going right:

If something goes wrong:

Edit	
Undo Typing	Ctrl+Z
Repeat Typing	Ctrl+Y

Save

Save your work to your hard drive (or wherever you usually save your work). To avoid accidentally over-writing your work, give your files different names than the ones that are on the CD.

Help With the Blinking Cursor Syndrome

If you're stuck on what to write about, just make up something for practice. Step 3, page 25, will help give you ideas for news stories. In addition, the planning you'll do in Step 1 will guide you in basic decisions about what to include.

A Quick Look at How You'll Use These Designs

Scroll back up to the top of page one on your screen. You've probably already noticed the questions on the screen. These questions are designed so that, when you answer them, you automatically build a newsletter article. Go ahead and give it a quick try here.

Place your cursor at the end of "When did it or will it happen?" and press Return or Enter. You'll see your cursor flashing in a new line as shown below.

Ignore the headline (Subject of news…) for now and start by answering the first question, "What is the most important thing that has happened since the last newsletter?" Continue through all of the other questions and answer those that apply (ignore those that don't).

What's Happening?

Name of the event

When will it happen?
Where will it happen?
Why is it important to readers?
How to sign up.

What's New?

Subject of news + action created

What is the most important thing that has happened since the last newsletter or will happen soon? What do readers need to know about it? What does it involve? What changes will it cause? What is being said about it? Why is it important to readers? Why did it happen?

Who is affected by the story? Who caused it to happen? How will it affect you or your readers? How will it benefit them? How did it happen? Where did it or will it happen? When did it or will it happen?

Tell readers who to call for more information or what action to take.

What's New?

Subject of news + action created

What is the most important thing that has happened since the last newsletter or will happen soon? What do readers need to know about it? What does it involve? What changes will it cause? What is being said about it? Why is it important to readers? Why did it happen?

Who is affected by the story? Who caused it to happen? How will it affect you or your readers? How will it benefit them? How did it happen? Where did it or will it happen? When did it or will it happen?

Newsletter Resources is releasing a new book called *Quick & Easy Newsletters*. Five years in the making, this book helps people create a newsletter in an afternoon. It's designed for use with MS-Word, WordPerfect and MS-Works. This product was created for those who've wanted to do a newsletter for a long time but didn't have the time or want to learn how to use a desktop publishing program.

Now, anyone with access to a computer and a photocopier can do a newsletter. The book is written by Elaine Floyd with the help of Susan Todd. It will be available at the end of this month through newsletter seminar companies and book stores.

Call (800) 264-6305 for more information on the book.

Place your cursor at the end of the second paragraph and press return. This holds the font and size from the previous paragraph. Answer the questions above the cursor to create a sample news article.

When you're finished, delete the questions listed above the news article you've written.

What's New?

Subject of news + action created

Newsletter Resources is releasing a new book called *Quick & Easy Newsletters*. Five years in the making, this book helps people create a newsletter in an afternoon. It's designed for use with MS-Word, WordPerfect and MS-Works. This product was created for those who've wanted to do a newsletter for a long time but didn't have the time or want to learn how to use a desktop publishing program.

Now, anyone with access to a computer and a photocopier can do a newsletter. The book is written by Elaine Floyd with the help of Susan Todd. It will be available at the end of this month through newsletter seminar companies and book stores.

Call (800) 264-6305 for more information on the book.

Changing Text in Gray Bars

If you want to change the text in the section heads (see Step 3), double click on the gray bars and follow the instructions for changing the tagline (see Setting Up the Nameplate below.). The text in the section heads should be centered (in MS Draw), but the bars themselves can be left aligned (in Works).

The text in the body paragraphs should be fully justified. To justify text, click on Paragraph under the Format menu. Click on Indents and Alignment and click on Justified. The headlines, action lines and any question and answer columns or trivia columns you use should be left aligned.

Setting Up the Nameplate

Your newsletter will be two or three columns, but the nameplate section is one column. Because column format applies to the entire document in Works, the nameplate is a separate document.

To complete Step 2: Newsworthy Names (page 19), open the file called "newsname.wps." Save the file under a new name. Keep the original document intact and make your changes under the new name you've created. Under the View menu, go to Zoom and adjust the level until you can see the full width of the document on the screen (try 75%). Under the View menu again, select Page Layout.

Tip:

For a better feel for the Works files on the disk, print this document and any of the other design documents in the Works directory. See page 14 and 15 for recommendations on which designs to use.

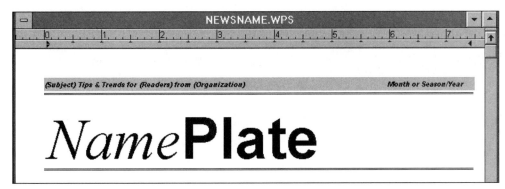

The Works file newsname.wps.

If NamePlate is Too High:

If the words "Name Plate" are shifted up into the horizontal bars on your screen, go to the Format menu and select Font and Style. Change the Position to Subscript to lower the text.

IMPORTANT:

This book is not a replacement for your MS-Works manual, Help screens or technical support. Please refer to those sources with questions that deal with the software's operation.

The tagline has a gray box around it that was created in Microsoft Draw. To customize the tagline, double click on the gray bar and Microsoft Draw will open. (If you single click on the gray bar instead of double clicking, you can accidentally move or resize it. If this happens, click on Undo under the Edit menu.)

The box and text are both selected when MS-Draw opens, so click somewhere on the screen other than on the gray bar to unselect them. Double click on the bar and the the words will be highlighted (most of the bar will turn white when the words are highlighted). Select the words you want to replace and type in the words you want (the words that have been selected will turn blue).

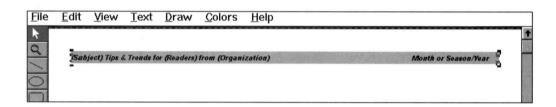

Replace "Month or Season/Year" with the correct date. MS-Draw does not have tabs, so you'll have to use the space bar to move the date to the right margin. Position it one or two spaces from the right margin.

When you are finished customizing the tagline, click on the screen to unselect the gray bar. Under File, click on Exit and Return to (document name). MS Draw will ask if you want to update your document. Click on yes.

Change the words "NamePlate" to your custom nameplate (see Step 2). The word "Name" is in Times New Roman italic, 72 point type, "Plate" is in Arial bold, 72 point type.

Print and save your new nameplate, making sure to have given it a different name than "newsname.wps." It's ready to be trimmed and taped (the old-fashioned way) to your document. Close the file.

You're finished with the tour of MS-Works.

Go to Step 1: Pain-Free Planning

 page 7

Inserting Clip Art and Graphics

To add a graphic to your newsletter, click on ClipArt under the Insert menu and choose from the clip art that came with MS-Works. Note that Some versions of Works cannot convert the clip art or cartoons that are included with the *Quick and Easy Newsletters* kit.

In Works 4.0, to use the clip art on the CD, under the Insert menu, select Drawing. MS-Draw will open. Under File, select Import Picture. Go to the CD and select a picture. Once you're back in MS-Draw, under the File menu, select Exit and Return.

News Word Selector

HELP FILES

(The text in italics notes the specific markets, newsletter types or audiences that certain words work well with.)

A

about …
abstract
account
access
acknowledgements
achievers
activists *(non-profits)*
addendum *(legal, accounting)*
advantage
advisor *(consultant)*
advocate *(non-profits)*
affiliate *(teambuilding)*
agent *(travel, insurance, real estate)*
applause *(employee)*
accolades *(employee)*
accomplishments *(employee)*
alert
ambassador
announcement
announcer
answer
anthem
articles
awakening

B

ballistic *(younger audiences)*
banner
bargain
basics
beacon
beat *(employee)*
bell
benchmark *(quality, teambuilding)*
benedictions *(church)*
benefactor

benefits
bend/bent
best *(employee)*
blabber/blurt *(employee)*
blessings *(church, nonprofit)*
blitz *(sales)*
blueprint
booster *(school, association, club)*
bonus
briefings
briefs
breakthroughs
breeze
bridge *(employee, non-profits)*
broadcast
browse
bullet
bulletin *(church, club)*
bullhorn
buzz

C

cable
call *(church, non-profit)*
calling card *(sales)*
calendar
capsule
caption
catchwords
catalyst *(non-profit)*
champion
chime *(health & wellness)*
channel
charter
chat
chatter
chorus, choir *(church)*
check
check-up *(health)*
chronicle
circuit *(employee)*
circular *(quality, employee)*
citizen *(community, neighborhood)*

classified(s)
clips
column
compass
compendium
concepts
conduit *(builder)*
coach *(consulting)*
coalition *(neighborhood, activist)*
code
comments
communicator
communique
companion
connection(s)
consultant
consumer
contemplations
conversations
conveyor *(manufacturing, industrial)*
council *(community)*
counsel
counselor
courier
course
copy
credits *(employee, volunteer)*
creed *(church)*
crusader *(non-profits, church)*
currents
cutting edge

D

daily *(employee, Web)*
dash
data
dateline
debuts
decision *(sales)*
declaration *(employee, non-profit)*
deductions *(accounting, tax)*
delegate *(advocacy)*
delicacies *(grocery, restaurant)*

delights *(food)*
depot
destination(s) *(travel)*
developments *(construction)*
devotions *(church)*
dialog
digest
difference
directions *(non-profit, travel)*
disciple *(church)*
discussion
dispatch
distractions *(community, travel)*
distributor *(distributors)*
distinctions
doings
doorways *(alternative medicine)*
doubletakes
dreams *(financial planning)*
dwellings *(literary)*

E

ear
echo
edge
elite *(employee)*
embark *(travel)*
emblem
emphasis
enchantments *(retail)*
enlighten *(church)*
enterprises
enthusiast *(association, club)*
envoy *(travel)*
epigram/epigraph
epiphany *(church)*
essence *(health)*
essentials *(retail)*
etc.
events
examiner
examples
excellence *(employee, quality)*
excerpts
exclamations
experience
expertise
experts *(professional practices)*
explorer *(travel)*
express
expressions
extra

extreme *(younger audiences)*
eye
eyeopener

F

facets
facts *(fax)*
faithful *(church)*
family *(employee, community)*
fan *(sports, association, club)*
fanatic *(hobby, sports, club)*
fanfare *(employee)*
FAQs
fashions *(retail)*
favorites
fax
features
feedback *(employee, customer)*
fellowship *(church)*
files
findings *(retailers, consultants)*
...first
fish stories
flash
flavor(s) *(restaurant)*
fleet *(employee)*
flock *(church)*
focus
fold
folks *(employee)*
follower *(church, association)*
follow-up
footprints *(church)*
footsteps
forecast
forefront
foresight
foreword
force *(salesforce, dealers)*
format
formula *(technical)*
fortune *(financial planning)*
forum
411 *(younger audiences)*
friend(s) *(neighborhood, non-profit)*
frenzy *(younger audiences)*
front porch *(real estate)*
funds *(financial planning)*
future
FYI

G

gab
galore
gallery
gateways
gathering *(church)*
gazette
gems
generations *(financial planning)*
get ahead
getaways *(travel)*
gifts *(non-profit)*
giveaways
glance(s)
glimpse
globe *(travel)*
glory *(church, employee)*
goals
goings on
goodbuys *(retail)*
gossip *(employee)*
grab bag *(employee, retail)*
grassroots *(non-profit, clubs)*
greenlight
greetings
...gram
growth
guardian *(non-profit, church)*
guest *(hotel)*
guide
guru

H

happenings
harbor *(non-profits, community)*
hardcore *(younger audiences)*
harvest *(church, financial)*
haywire
headlines
healthbeat *(healthcare)*
headstart
heartbeats *(healthcare)*
help
herald
heritage *(community, museums,
     collectors, hobbyists)*
hideaways *(travel, real estate)*
highlights
highwire
highways *(travel)*
hints
hodgepodge
holdings *(financial, real estate)*

homage
homepage
homespun ...
hotline
horizons *(travel, financial)*
hubbub *(employee)*
hullabaloo
humanist *(non-profit)*
humanitarian *(non-profit)*

I

ideal
ideas
ignition
illumination *(church)*
images
impressions
impact
imprint
in brief
information
informer
ink
inklings
inside/insider
insights
intelligence
interludes
investor *(financial)*
issues
items
itinerary *(travel)*

J

jargon
jaunt *(travel)*
jazz
joiner *(association)*
junctions
jottings
journal
journeys
jubilee *(Southern)*
jurist *(legal)*

K

keepers
keepsake *(retail)*
kernel
keynotes
keystone *(construction)*
kibitzer
kudos *(employee, volunteer, association)*

L

landscape *(travel, real estate)*
leader
leaflet
letter
leverage
levity
line
lingo
link
list
listing *(real estate)*
litany *(church)*
look-out
loop
low-down
luminary *(consultant, financial)*

M

magic/magician
mailer
malarkey
manager
mania
mantra *(New Age)*
map
market
mastermind
matters of fact
matters
maximize
meandorings *(travel)*
measures *(safety, quality, financial)*
medal *(employee)*
memo
mentions *(employee, association)*
mentor
merchant
meridian *(alternative medicine)*
message
messenger
ministry *(church)*
miracles *(non-profit, church)*
misnomer *(bookstore, writer)*
mission *(church)*
money
moneyguide
monitor
monthly
morsels
mystique *(New Age, alternative medicine)*

N

phonetic:
know-how
knick-knack

narrator
navigator
necessities
neighbor *(community)*
nestegg
network *(association, business)*
news
news brief
newsline
newsworthy...
nitty-gritty
notables *(employee)*
notes
noteworthy...
notice
now
nuts & bolts

O

oasis
observer
occasions *(event planner, retailer)*
odds & ends
offbeat
offline
online
opinion *(financial)*
opportunities
options *(financial, stock)*
orbits *(employee)*
outburst
outlook
output *(quality, employee)*
outreach
out-write
ovation *(speaker, employee)*
overture
overview

P

page
pandemonium
panorama
paper
partner
passages
passing notes
passport *(travel)*

passwords *(travel, computer)*
pathways
peeks/peaks
peers
penant
people *(employee)*
perennial
perspective
peruser
petition *(advocacy)*
pilot
planner
platform *(political)*
plus
point blank
point of sale *(sales, retail)*
pointers
pontifications
possibilities
postmark
potpourri
practitioner
predictions
premiums
press
presto
pride
printout
proceedings *(legal)*
producer
professional
progress
profile
prophesy
prose
prospectus
prototype
proverbs *(church)*
pullout
pulpit *(church)*
pulse *(employee)*
pursuit(s)

Q

Q&A
quality…
quantifier
quarterly
querry
quest
quick takes

quill
quips
quiz
quotes *(financial, too)*

R

rabbit ears
radical *(younger audiences)*
radio
ramblings
rant *(younger audiences)*
rap *(younger audiences)*
rapport *(internal)*
rave *(younger audiences)*
reader
readings
read me
recipe *(restaurant, grocery)*
record
red letter/read letter
reflections
refrains
regular
reminder
relay
release
repartee
report
reporter
resource
results
review(s)
…in review
rewards
rhythms
riches
roll call *(employee)*
roster *(employee)*
roundup
route
rumors
the rundown
Rx

S

Sabbath *(church)*
safari
salute *(employee)*
sampler *(safety, quality)*
sanctuary *(church, non-profit)*
satellite
… savvy
scene

scoop
scope
score
scout
scuttlebutt
scholar
seasonings *(quarterly newsletters, retail, grocery, restaurants)*
secrets
selections *(retail, museum)*
seller
sentinel
sheet
shenanigans
shepherd *(church)*
shindig
shorts
signal
signature
sign-up
sketches
skimmings
smalltalk *(employee, neighborhood)*
smatterings
smiles
snapshots
soapbox
solutions
sound bites
soundings
source
speaking of…
speaks
specialist
specialties *(retail, grocery)*
specs *(optometry, manufacturer)*
spectrum
spectulations/spectulator *(financial)*
spellbinder
spin
spinoff
spirit
splash
spotlight
stages *(employee)*
standard *(quality, safety)*
stats
story/stories
straight talk
strategies
stuff *(younger audiences)*
success
summary

summit
sundries
supplement
supplier
supporter
surveyor
synopsis
synthesis
systems

T

tactics
takes
taking stock
talents
tales
talk
tallies
tangents
target
tattler
team
techniques
tempo
temptations
testament *(church)*
testimony *(legal)*
thoughts
threads
ticket *(travel)*
tidbits
tidings
ties
times
tip off
tips
to-and-fro *(travel)*
toasts
today
tokens
toolbox
tools
trades
traveler
treasures *(retail, investment)*
trends
trifles
tunes
twist

U

unifier
uniter
update
upfront
uplift
uplink
ups and downs *(stocks)*
upshort
upstart
upswing
uptake
up-to-date
upturn

V

value(s)
vantage
vault
variety
vehicle
vendor
ventures
verbatim
verdict *(legal)*
vernacular
verses
veteran
vibrations
viewpoint
views
vignette(s) *(speakers)*
villager *(community)*
vim & vigor
vine
virtuoso
visible
vision
visionary
vistas
viva …
voice
volume
volunteer
vote/voter *(political)*

W

wagon *(quality, employee)*
wanderings *(travel)*
watch
watchdog *(activist, non-profit)*
watchword
water cooler *(employee)*

watering hole
wave
way
wealth
web
weigh-in
welcome
wellspring *(New Age)*
whims
whispers
whiz
whodunit *(employee, volunteer)*
whoopee
windfall
window
wire
wisdom
wish list
wishing well
wit
wit & wisdom
witness *(church)*
wiz
wizard
wonders
word
word for word
working capital
works
worship *(church)*
world
worldwide
wrap-up
write-up

X

x-ray
see also z and ex for phonetic matches

Y

yak
yearnings
yields
yippee

Z

zeal
zest
zone
zoom

HELP FILES

Section Headings

NEWS

What's New?
In the News
Top of the News
Did You Know?
Did You Hear?
The Newsdesk
Tell Me More
The Latest News
At a Glance
What's New?
Check It Out
What's Up?
From the Newswire
Hot Off the Presses
Followups
The Media and the Message
Stop the Presses
Trend Watch
Must Reads
The Toolbox
Readables
Notables
The Round Table
Heads Up
News and Notes
New and Noteworthy
For the Record
Facts and Footnotes
In the Spotlight
News to Use
Shorts
At Issue Here
Briefs
In Brief
Profiles, Pointers & Proclamations

Highlights
News and Views
News and Reviews
Quick Reads
Tidbits
Bits and Pieces
Bits-n-Pieces
Bits and Bytes
Sound Bites
The Nitty-Gritty
Much Ado About Something
Nuts-n-Bolts
Updates
That's Good to Know
News, Views, Reviews, To-do's
Resources
News and Issues
Tips, Tools and Trends
What, Where, When, Why, Who, and How
On the Record
Checkmarks
Hotline
Issues
Fit to Print
FYI
Get the Scoop
What-Nots
What's Here?
What Have You?
What's What?
What's Tops?
What's Hot?
What's Hot? What's Not?
What's New With You?
What Gives? (non-profit)
What's Notable?

What's the Good Word?
What's the Point?

PEOPLE

Who's News?
What's the Buzz?
What's the Scoop?
What's the Story?
What Do You Know?
What's all the Hubbub, Bub?
What's Your Sign?
What's Your Number?
What's Important?
What's it all Mean?
What's Your Impression?
Who's New?

Profiles

Rising Stars
Star Performers
In the Spotlight
In the Limelight
Curtain Calls
Bursting With Pride
Our Pride and Joy
The Center of Attention
Behind the Scenes
Standing Ovations
Bravo!
Making a Name
Getting Noticed
Introducing ...
Meet 'Em and Greet 'Em
Putting a Face With a Name
Where Credit is Due
You're the Tops
Apples of Our Eye

Worthy of Esteem
Success Stories
Praiseworthy
Honorable Mentions
Staff Spotlight
Employee Excellence
Biographies
People, Places and Things
Grab Bag
From the Grapevine
Around the Water Cooler
News from the Pews *(chuches)*

Also:
Use alone or look for alliterations with company or organization name:
Bigshots, Bigwigs, Celebrates, Celebrity, Compliments, Excellence, Fame, Famous, Features, Headliners, Heroes, Highlights, Notables, Portraits, Profiles, Sensations, Snapshots, Stand-outs, Stars, Superlatives, Superstars, Talent, Top-Notch, Winners

Letters
Feedback
We're Listening
Letter Perfect
Verbatim
Mailbag
Mailbox
Maildrop
The Voice Box
Voiceovers
Postings
Postmarks
From the Grapevine
Mail Matters
Pass Us a Note
Readers Reply
Readers Speak
Readers Respond
Reader Response
Customer Comments
Hearsay *(legal)*
Reader Round Table

What's on Your Mind?
The Suggestion Card
Your Turn
From the Pews *(church)*

EDUCATION
Questions and answers
Q&A
FAQs
What Works?
Dear [company name] ...
Frequently Asked Questions
Asked & Answered *(legal)*
You Asked For It
You've Been Asking
We Want to Know
You Want to Know
Information, Please
Since You Asked
Backtalk
Input and Output
Ask the Experts
Soundings
Sound Bytes
The Sounding Board

Editorials
On My Mind
In My Opinion
In My View
News from *[organization]*
[name] Says ...
Take It From Me
Take It From the Top
A Letter From *[name]*
President's Corner
President's Pen
From the Soapbox
From the Pulpit
From Behind the Desk
From *[name's]* Keyboard
Welcome from *[organization]*
Sage Advice
From the Mountaintop
The Presidential Address
[name's] Sermon
Memo from *[name]*

Presidential Postings
Presidential Predictions
Presidential Press
Presidential Proverbs
Presidential Profundity
Chat From the Chair
Chairperson's Channel
Chairperson's Checkup

Greetings and Salutations
Editorial Echos
Editorial Ear
Editorial Eye
Editorial Expressions
The Op-Ed Section
Perspectives
Insights

EVENTS
What's Happening?
What's Going On?
What's Up Doc?
What's Up?
What's Next?
Section/Calendar Names
Wonderings and Wanderings
Goings On
Get Up and Go
Around Town
Reminders
Countdown to ...

ENTERTAINMENT
What's Been Said?
What's Wise?
What's My Line?
What's So Funny?
What's Inspiring?
What If?
What's Worth Repeating?
What's the Answer?
What's Cookin'?
Fun Facts
Sound Bites
Quotable Quotes
Did You Know?
What's the Answer?

The Top 10 Reasons
Brain Teasers
Food for Thought

ADS, OFFERS, TEASERS

What's the Deal?
What's In It For You?
Quick Reply
You Asked For It, You Got It
Freebies
Call Today For a Free *(offer)*
Try the New *(product)* Risk Free
Mention This Newsletter and
Receive a Free Gift
Inside: Annual Market Forecast
Call *(phone number)* for a Free
Catalog
Check Out Our Web Site at
(www.whatever.com)
Call For a Free Sample of
(product)
For Members Only
For the First Time ...
Our Biggest Sale Ever
From Our Family to Yours
Editor's Tool Box
Opportunity Knocks
Wish List

What's on the CD?

Cartoons:

art / attitude.pcx

art / journey.pcx

art / the tour.pcx

Page Element:

shdowbox.pcx, shdowbox.eps

Clip Art:

arrived.pcx

balloon.pcx

bkborder.pcx

bkontape.pcx

bkaward.pcx

bookcal.pcx

booknl.pcx

bookrev.pcx

briefs.pcx

broadcast.pcx

calendar.pcx

call2.pcx

call2.pcx

CD.pcx

Cofee&do.pcx

Cofeecup.pcx

coming.pcx

deadline.pcx

facts.pcx

fanmail.pcx

fax.pcx

faxnews.pcx

featured.pcx

frig.pcx

gift.pcx

giftcert.pcx

giftwrap.pcx

idea.pcx

lightning.pcx

lineofbk.pcx

list.pcx

mail.pcx

mailbox.pcx

message.pcx

microphn.pcx

minutes.pcx

news.pcx

newslink.pcx

notepad.pcx

notes.pcx

open.pcx

pencil.pcx

question.pcx

quill.pcx

quotes.pcx

readgrp.pcx

recyclogo.pcx

reminder.pcx

reviews.pcx

rubrstmp.pcx

save.pcx

saverth.pcx

saverth2.pcx

scroll.pcx

signings.pcx

speaker.pcx

stopsign.pcx

storyhr1.pcx

storyhr2.pcx

survey.pcx

tack.pcx

treasury.pcx

trumpet.pcx

wedding.pcx

winner.pcx

Quotations

MS-Word: *quotes.doc*
WordPerfect: *quotes.wpf*
MS-Works: *quotes.wps*

"We make a living by what we get, but we make a life by what we give."
—Winston Churchill

"Courage is resistance to fear, mastery of fear—not absence of fear."
—Mark Twain

"Worry and Faith are bitter enemies; when Worry enters, Faith goes out the back door."
—J. Melvin Gibby

"In the long run men hit only what they aim at."
—Henry David Thoreau

"This world is but canvas to our imaginations."
—Henry David Thoreau

"To him whose elastic and vigorous thought keeps pace with the sun, the day is a perpetual morning."
—Henry David Thoreau

"You are the same today as you'll be in five years except for two things, the people you meet and the books you read."
—Charlie "Tremendous" Jones

"I value the friend who for me finds time on his calendar, but I cherish the friend who for me does not consult his calendar.
—Robert Brault

"Nothing I never said ever did me any harm."
—Calvin Coolidge

"By the time a man realizes that maybe his father was right, he usually has a son who thinks he's wrong."
—Charles Wadsworth

"If opportunity doesn't knock, build a door."
—Milton Berle

"If lady luck fails to show at your door, pay her a visit."
—J. Melvin Gibby

"Motivation is what gets you started, habit is what keeps you going."
—Jim Ryun

"Obstacles are things a person sees when he takes his eyes off the goal."
—E. Joseph Cossman

"It is not true that nice guys finish last. Nice guys are winners before the game ever starts."
—Addison Walker

"You can never grow until you push yourself past the point of exhaustion."
—General Patton

"If I had eight hours to chop down a tree, I'd spend six sharpening my ax."
—Abraham Lincoln

"Nothing in fine print is ever good news."
—Andy Rooney

"The surest way to be late is to have plenty of time."
—Leo Kennedy

The trouble with being punctual is that nobody's there to appreciate it."
—Franklin P. Jones

"Nothing makes a person more productive than the last minute."
—Unknown

"Every act of creation is first of all an act of destruction."
—Pablo Picasso

"A man's errors are his portals of discovery."
—James Joyce

"50% of success is believing you can. Simply put, you become what you think about."
—Jeffrey Gitomer

Hint:
You can use the clip art image quotes.pcx along with your quotes.

Trivia

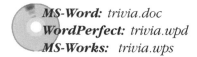

MS-Word: *trivia.doc*
WordPerfect: *trivia.wpd*
MS-Works: *trivia.wps*

ANIMALS

Which animal has no vocal cords?
Giraffes

How far away can you hear a lion's roar?
Five miles

What is the only cat that can't retract its claws?
Cheetah

How many flowers does it take for bees to collect enough nectar to make one tablespoon of honey?
Two thousand flowers

What percentage of all forms of life that have ever existed on earth are now extinct?
95

How many mosquitoes are there in the U.S. every year?
About ten trillion

GEOGRAPHY

What are the two mobile national monuments in the U.S.?
The San Francisco cable cars and the St. Charles streetcar line in New Orleans

What is the only country whose name begins with "A" but doesn't end in "A?"
Afghanistan

US Interstates running north and south have odd numbers; those running east and west have even numbers.

What is the most northern, eastern and western state?
Alaska

How many meteors have hit the earth in its history?
At least one million

How fast does the earth move at its equator?
About 1000 miles an hour

How many earthquakes does the earth have in a year?
About 50,000

How many of the smallest states could fit into Alaska?
21

What is the only state the borders on only one state?
Maine

What three cities are named exactly after the state they're located in?
Maine, ME; New York, NY: Wyoming, WY

What do Paris, France, and Cedar Rapids, Iowa, have in common?
They are the only cities with their governments on an island.

What is the only continent without reptiles or snakes?
Antarctica

What do the national anthems of the United States and the Netherlands have in common?
Neither anthem mentions the country's name

What is the only state bordered on both east and west entirely by rivers?
Iowa

Which state has the most personalized license plates?
Illinois

What is the record for the most snowfall in a day?
78 inches on February 7, 1916, in Alaska

PEOPLE

Men with what hair color are most likely to go bald?
Red

How much hair does the human body produce in a lifetime?
About 350 miles

How many shades of color are humans capable of distinguishing?
About 300,000

Who blinks more, men or women?
Women (almost twice as often)

What is the national average ACT score?
17

What's the average life span of a tastebud?
Ten days

What is the other claim-to-fame of the inventor of liquid paper (White Out)?
She is the mother of Mike Nesmith of the Monkees

SPORTS/GAMES

How many times must a deck of cards be shuffled in order for the cards to be mixed up properly?
Seven

What sport has been the subject of the most Hollywood films?
Boxing

What sport has the highest ratio of officials to participants?
Tennis, with 13 officials for 2 players

More money is printed daily for the game of Monopoly than is printed by the U.S. Treasury.

Who is the only person to be elected to both the baseball and football Halls of Fame?
Cal Hubbard

What is the total length of time a golf ball is on the face of the club during an 18-hole game?
Less than half a second

What are the only seven teams in the four major US professional sports whose nicknames do not end in S?
(basketball) Utah Jazz, Miami Heat, Orlando Magic
(baseball) Boston Red Sox, Chicago White Sox
(hockey) Colorado Avalanche, Tampa Bay Lightning
(football) none

Who was the only person to letter in four sports at UCLA?
Jackie Robinson (who supposedly liked baseball the least of the four)

What is the oldest sporting event in the US?
The Kentucky Derby

What is the second oldest sporting even in the US?
The Westminster Kennel Club Dog Show

What is the only city in the U.S. with three sports teams that all wear the same colors?
Pittsburgh, PA

Who are the only two people in the baseball Hall of Fame who had nothing to do with baseball?
Abbott and Costello

ENTERTAINMENT

What is the most filmed book of all time?
Dracula

What is the name of the sorcerer in Disney's Fantasia?
Yensid (Disney backwards)

What is the only movie to have its sequel released the same year?
King Kong (sequel - Son of Kong), 1933

What is Barbie's full name?
Barbara Millicent Roberts

What would Barbie's measurements be if she were life-sized?
39-23-33

In The Wizard of Oz, what is Dorothy's last name?
Gale

MUSIC

What key is the dial tone of a normal telephone?
F

What key do most American car horns beep in?
F

What is the song The Merry-Go Round is Broken Down better known as?
The Looney Tunes theme song

WORDS

What is the only letter of more than one syllable?
W

In Chinese, the words for crisis and opportunity are the same.

What is the only English word with two synonyms which are antonyms of each other?
Cleave, which has adhere and separate as synonyms

What is unusual about the words stewardesses and reverberated?
They are the longest words that can be typed using only the left hand.
Lollipop is the longest word that can be typed using only the right hand, and skepticism is the longest word that requires alternating hands

What is the only word that consists of two letters, each used three times?
Deeded

What is the origin of the product name Gatorade?
It was developed at the University of Florida, whose team nickname is the Gators

From what language does the word robot originate?
Czech/Slovak

What word has the most consonants in a row?
Latchstring

What's the highest scoring word in the game of Scrabble?
Quartzy (which will score 164 points on a tripe-word square with the Z on a double-letter square)

What is the only 15-letter word that can be spelled without repeating a letter?
Uncopyrightable

What is the origin of the chess term checkmate?
From the Persian phrase sha mat, which means "the king is dead"

Religion

Which two books of the Bible do not mention the word God?
Esther and Song of Solomon

What is the longest chapter in the Bible?
Psalm 119

What is the shortest verse in the Bible?
Jesus wept

Hint:

You can use the clip art image question.pcx along with your trivia.

Filler Articles

MS-Word: *filler.doc*
WordPerfect: *filler.wpd*
MS-Works: *filler.wps*

Improve your telephone persona

We all spend a lot of time on the phone—so much so that it's easy to take for granted. Use these techniques to maintain a friendly, professional phone manner.

- Answer before the third ring.
- Smile when you speak on the phone—it shows in your voice.
- State your name when you answer.
- Repeat customer questions back to them to make sure you've understood.
- Ask customers to call back if they have other questions.

Whether customers are in front of you, across town, or across the country, always project a customer-friendly, service-minded attitude.

Protect your voice like an opera star

If you're prone to losing your voice, try these tips from public speaker Joanna Slan.

1) Try Riccola lozenges. Eucalyptus lozenges (such as Halls) are too harsh on the throat.
2) Take lots of vitamin C.
3) Drink plenty of water--especially before and during plane rides.
4) Don't let steam from the bathroom into the hotel rooms. It spreads mold spores.
5) DO take long steamy showers at home if you feel a cold coming on.

Cold-Ease, while hard on the stomach, helps ward off colds.
6) Hot water and honey is a staple, especially with a bit of peppermint tea.
7) Avoid dairy products and drink pineapple juice.
And, of course, you can always just talk less.

Make the Internet work for you

The Internet can be an invaluable research tool, but it can also be a huge waste of time. Use these tips to avoid getting stuck in Cyberspace.

- Get on the network early in the day to avoid high-traffic times.
- Upgrade your modem to at least 28.8 bps.
- Don't get sidetracked by interesting but irrelevant sites.
- Read the "help" files for the search engine you use most often.
- Bookmark useful sites for future reference.
- If there's reading material you've been meaning to get to, glance through it while waiting for large sites to load.
- Turn off the graphics capabilities on your browser for really efficient searches.

With a little patience and a little common sense, you can make the Internet into an efficient and powerful asset to your business.

Uncle Sam provides fast, free research

Tap into the U.S. Census data online at http://www.census.gov. You'll find information on the current U.S. and world populations, population projections, current economic indicators and more. Learn the top industries in each region or county. Find out the average household income, size and other facts nationwide or by state or county. Detailed maps and summaries are available for downloading. Since it's government-provided and funded, you can use any of the information or graphics copyright free.

Hold onto your price reduction

A 15-year study by The Vass Company found that 90 percent of all sellers volunteer a price reduction without being asked. Their conclusion—sellers do not believe in the value of their product or service. In addition, 80 percent failed to close the sale when the buyer was ready.

How to reduce day-to-day stress

If you're like most people, your day is more hectic than you'd like. Try the following stress-relieving tips:

- Take deep breaths when you feel tense.
- Place a reminder on your desk and in your car to sit up straight. Poor posture makes it difficult for the body to take in oxygen.
- Listen to relaxing music. Light jazz, classical or mood music slows the heart rate.
- Keep lavender oil handy. Rub a bit into a handkerchief. Breathe from the handkerchief from time to time.
- Get regular massages to relieve the body of pent-up muscle tension.
- Complete important tasks early in the day to avoid worrying about them later.

How to instill a love of reading in your child

In this age of cable TV, computers and video games, parents often wonder what they can do to teach their children to enjoy books. The most important thing you can do is to share their reading with them. Try these tips.

- Read to younger children and with older ones every day.
- Make sure your children see you reading.
- Vary your reading to include magazines, books and newspapers.
- Discuss books with your children; ask them what happened in their stories.
- Take children to the library or to bookstores.
- Encourage children to join book clubs or reading groups.
- Treat reading as a reward, not as homework.

If kids learn to love reading early, the habit will stay with them throughout their lives.

Rest one day in seven

Ancient sanctions prohibited most activities, even traveling, on a weekly day of rest. Could you not drive somewhere for one whole day? Public speaker Rita Risser has a challenge for you. Could you not think about work for 24 hours? Try enjoying a day of reading books, meditating, strolling around the neighborhood, playing with the dog, talking with friends, playing music, drawing, writing letters and cuddling loved ones. This weekly day of rest is more relaxing than two weeks of vacation.

Play tourist in your home town

Does your town have a great museum, zoo, park or cultural center? Do you only visit these places when you're entertaining out-of-town guests? We all look forward to going to other cities to enjoy tourist attractions but often overlook these opportunities at home. Buy a guidebook for your city—look especially for books which specialize in "off the beaten path" attractions—and pretend to be a visitor. You can take several of these "mini-vacations" a month, and you'll learn more about your home town and enjoy it more.

How to maintain an exercise routine

- Work out at the same time every day.
- Exercise with someone else and motivate each other.
- Exercise in the morning—you're less likely to find excuses to skip it and your metabolism will be higher all day.
- Choose a form of exercise you enjoy; think of it as play, not work.
- Get more sleep; you need it when you're working out a lot and you'll perform better.
- Vary the types of exercise you do.
- Play basketball, soccer, tennis or other games that let you exercise in a competitive but social environment.
- Have a goal such as weight loss, muscle growth or improving a personal best.

Eat nutritious meals so your diet and exercise routine work together.

Set your luggage apart from the crowd

Avoid the nightmare many travelers have had when someone pulls their lookalike bag off the carousel. Travel expert and author of Wing Tips, Allen Klein, says to buy bright-colored luggage, paste bright stickers on it or wrap it with a bright-colored luggage strap. Luggage straps have the added benefit of being a hindrance against pilferage and provide insurance for faulty locks.

How to avoid jet lag on overnight flights

- Cut out all caffeine after 10 a.m. on the day of your flight.
- Drink water all day and avoid carbonated beverages.
- Keep your pre-flight meal light.

Once you're on the plane:

- Set your watch according to the time zone you're traveling to.
- Tell the flight attendant that you want to sleep the entire flight.
- Shut your eyes and relax until breakfast, even if you don't fall asleep.

Step-by-step packing to reduce wrinkles

- Place tissue or plastic bags between each garment to let items slide rather than settle.
- Lay pants waistband to waistband with legs left outside suitcase (don't close it yet!)
- Fold blouses or shirts and place them face down.
- Turn suit jackets or blazers inside out, fold them and face them down.
- Fold the pants legs over the top.
- Add skirts, sweaters, socks and undergarments—all laid flat.
- Line the sides of the suitcase with shoes and cosmetics (both in plastic bags).
- Circle the inside circumference of the suitcase with belts.

Tips and trends for _____ **from** _____ _____

_____ _____

What's New?

What's Happening?

This form is **fillnews.pdf** on the CD.

What's Fun?

Who's New?

What Do You Know?

*This form is **fillnews.pdf** on the CD.*

"

"

Newsletter Necessities

Books & Booklets

Making Money Writing Newsletters
by Elaine Floyd
PaperDirect
www.paperdirect.com
(800) 272-7377

Marketing With Newsletters
by Elaine Floyd
PaperDirect
www.paperdirect.com
(800) 272-7377

Marketing Your Bookstore
With a Newsletter
by Elaine Floyd
EFG, Inc.
St. Louis, MO
(314) 353-6100

Newsletter Editor's Handbook
by Marvin Arth, Helen Ashmore &
Elaine Floyd
PaperDirect
www.paperdirect.com
(800) 272-7377

Publishing Newsletters
by Howard Penn Hudson
Newsletter Clearinghouse
www.newsletter-clearinghse.com
(800) 572-3451

You CAN Sell Ads
in Your Newsletter
Promotional Perspectives
www.dtp-cpr.com
(734) 994-0007

Publications on Design & Editing

Communication Briefings
www.briefings.com
(800) 915-0022

Editorial Eye
Editorial Experts
www.eeicom.com
(703) 683-0683

Fillers for Newsletters

First Draft
Ragan Communications
www2.ragan.com
(312) 335-0037

Ideas Unlimited
(800) 345-2611

NewslettersDirect
www.newslettersdirect.com
www.newsletterfillerscom
(303) 422-0726

Clip Art

Art for the Church
Communication Resources
Canton, OH
www.comresources.com
(800) 992-2144

ClickArt
T/Maker Company
graphics.software-directory.com/

Clip Art Series
Broderbund
www.broderbund.com
(800) 395-0277

Cliptures
Dream Maker Software
www.coolclipart.com
(303) 350-8557

Designer's Club
Dynamic Graphics Inc.
www.dgusa.com
(800) 255-8800

EyeWire
Image Club Graphics, Inc.
eyewire.com
(800) 661-9410

Images With Impact
3G Graphics
graphics.software-directory.com
(206) 774-3518

Cartoons

Comics Plus
United Media
www.unitedmedia.com
(800) 221-4816

Business & Safety Cartoons
by Ted Goff
P.O. Box 22679
Kansas City, MO 64113
www.tedgoff.com

Business and Computer Cartoons
by Randy Glasbergen
www.borg.com

Grantland Enterprises
Charlottesville, VA
www.grantland.net
(434) 964-1238

Dan Rosandich
Chassell, MI
www.gorp.com
(906) 482-6234

Brad Veley
339 E. Arch St.
Marquette, MI 49855
(906) 228-3229

Newsletter & Secretarial Skills Seminars

How to Design Eye-Catching
Brochures, Newsletters, Ads,
Reports
CareerTrack
www.careertrack.com
(800) 780-8476

Online Publications and Content
Training
Editorial Experts
Alexandria, VA
www.eeicommunications.com/
onlinetraining/catalog.htm
(703) 683-0683

Ragan Communications
212 W. Superior St.
Chicago, IL 60605
(312) 335-0037

How to Design Attention-
Grabbing Brochures, Catalogs,
Ads, Newsletters and Reports
SkillPath
Shawnee Mission, KS
www.skillpath.com
(800) 873-7545

Index

The Tour de Pants